CUBA:

RESTRUCTURING THE ECONOMY –

A CONTRIBUTION TO THE DEBATE

by

Julio Carranza Valdés

Luis Gutiérrez Urdaneta

Pedro Monreal González

Translated with Foreword by
Ruth Pearson

Institute of Latin American Studies
31 Tavistock Square, London WC1H 9HA

ILAS

Institute of Latin American Studies
School of Advanced Study
University of London

British Library Cataloguing-in-Publication Data
A catalogue record for this book is available
from the British Library

ISBN   1 900039 09 5

NOTES ON THE AUTHORS

Julio Carranza Valdés (La Habana, 1958). Economist. For several years sub-director and researcher at the Centro de Estudios sobre América (CEA) in Havana, Cuba. Profesor Adjunto in the Universidad de La Habana and in the Instituto Superior de Relaciones Internacionales de Cuba. Has written articles for academic journals in Cuba and abroad. Has been visiting professor in several universities and institutions in the United States, Europe and Latin America, and has participated in numerous international events.

Luis Gutiérrez Urdaneta (La Habana, 1957). Economist. For several years researcher at the Centro de Estudios sobre América (CEA) in Havana, Cuba. Previously worked as specialist and head of department of the Union of Enterprises in Havana. Also worked as civilian specialist in the Group on Business Improvement in the Armed Forces (Grupo de Perfeccionamiento Empresarial de las Fuerzas Armadas). Has given lectures and carried out research in universities in the United States and Latin America. Has written articles for national and overseas academic journals.

Pedro Monreal González (Guantánamo, 1958). Economist. For several years researcher at the Centro de Estudios sobre América (CEA) in Havana, Cuba. Profesor Adjunto in the Universidad de La Habana and in the Instituto Superior de Relaciones Internacionales de Cuba. Has written articles for national and overseas academic journals. Has been visiting professor and researcher in universities and institutions in the United States, Canada, Europe and Latin America, and has participated in numerous international events.

Ruth Pearson (London, 1945). Economist with 20 years experience working in Latin America. Much of her work has concerned gender analysis of economic policy, industrialisation and women's employment. Since 1994 has been researching micro level response to macro policy change in Cuba. She currently holds two posts – one at the School of Development Studies at the University of East Anglia and one as Professor of Women and Development at the Institute of Social Studies, the Hague.

CONTENTS

Foreword

The project of translating this book into English was conceived during a trip to Cuba at the beginning of January 1996. I have had the opportunity to monitor Cuba's transition since 1993 when the economy was living through the worst consequences of the abrupt and brutal de-linking from the trading blocks of Eastern Europe and the former Soviet Union and the tightening of the blockade on trade and credit imposed by the United States government.

I observed first hand some of the measures implemented by the Cuban Government which had led to the stemming of the abrupt economic decline which had accelerated since 1989, and the apparent restoration of positive growth rates of national product since 1993. As a visitor and researcher concerned with the impact of the crisis on household and community strategies, I had tracked the changes in the shortages of domestic electricity, the crisis in urban transport and the availability of consumer goods, especially food, toiletries and clothing, and the measures taken to deal with the problems in distribution and transportation, particularly the introduction of agricultural markets (for food products) and of industrial and artisanal markets. I had observed the growth in own-account activity and read about the steps taken by the government to update and expand the regulation of a thriving informal sector. This sector, or more specifically the self-employment sector, was previously part of the submerged economy. But as more people found it necessary to seek other employment as the result of rationalisation in state enterprises, the self-employed sector had ceased to be the counter-revolutionary black market and had become an essential element in absorbing redundant labour power. Even for those still employed in public enterprises and services, to seek additional income generating activities in retail trading, or domestic and restaurant services, was a rational response by households seeking to extend their livelihood strategies.[1]

The 1993-96 period witnessed a significant change in both the management and the performance of the Cuban economy. A number of key reforms, including in 1993 decentralisation of state-owned agricultural enterprises into UBPCs (a regulated network of workers' cooperatives) was followed in October 1994 by the opening of free agricultural markets (farmers' markets) which supplied a range of food products from the private cooperative, as well as the state sector, directly to consumers. With food security a major objective of the Revolution, which had up till then managed the crisis by strict consumer rationing resulting inevitably in an escalating illegal black market, other measures were proposed to increase agricultural productivity and production. Scarce inputs – imported spare parts, fertilisers, herbicides and fuel – were to be offset by reorganising production, increasing individual incentives for increasing production in key

---

[1]   See Ruth Pearson, 'Renegotiating the Reproductive Bargain: A Gender Analysis of Transition in Cuba', *Development and Change*, 1997.

commodities, changing cropping patterns, encouraging direct trade between different production units and exploring low input production techniques including organic pest control and inter-cropping. The shortage of labour, a chronic feature of Cuban agriculture since the early sugar harvest campaigns of the 1960s, was to be overcome by increasing self-provisioning not just by farmers but also by a range of Cuban enterprises and work places including educational and research institutes, health centres and hospitals, and the armed forces. In addition, under-employed or displaced urban workers were encouraged to re-locate to the countryside to work in agriculture under favourable conditions in terms of allocation of land. In view of the shortage of food in the capital, voluntary labour mobilisations were encouraged and rewarded in kind.

These measures achieved what few could have predicted: the revaluation of the Cuban currency, the peso. The availability of food and other goods purchasable in national currency decreased the incentive to hold and trade in dollars, which had been legal since June 1993. The parallel exchange rate fell from 130 pesos to the dollar in September 1993 to 25 pesos in January 1996.

The external constraints on the Cuban economy, squeezed between the escalating blockade of the USA and the demise of the trade and credit previously available from the Soviet bloc, were to be addressed by a sectoral policy which prioritised the tourist industry, traditional exports of sugar and nickel, and import –substituting measures including intensifying petroleum extraction and processing within the island. Joint ventures between state enterprises and foreign companies were extended from the priority export and import substitution sectors to the financial and domestic sectors of the economy.

The government also addressed the fiscal and monetary crisis of the economy. Administered prices in the 'free' agricultural and other markets soaked up a large proportion of the monetary overhung, which had built up over the years of controlled prices and declining commodities for purchase. Plans to introduce staged and progressive income taxes and sales taxes, as well as increases in charges for utilities and services supplied by the state, were part of a concerted policy package to reform public finances.

Enterprise reform – in terms of decentralisation, enterprise responsibility for obtaining and financing requisite inputs both imported and domestic, resource allocation according to efficiency and rationalisation and increased productivity of labour – were also part of the reform agenda of the government.

However, what had never been clear to me was how these different measures fitted into a clear plan for the restructuring of the Cuban economy. In January 1996 I was recommended by a range of people – Cuban academics, government officials, politicians, as well as foreign diplomats and investors – to read *Cuba: La restructuración de la economía: Una propuesta para el debate*. Indeed, this volume is the most comprehensive attempt by Cuban economists to explain how the different measures referred to above fit into a coherent programme aimed at restructuring the Cuban economy whilst maintaining the socialist objectives of the Revolution.

Having agreed to translate the volume, I completed the task in February 1996. However, in March 1996 Julio Carranza, one of the authors of the book, visited the Institute of Latin American Studies (ILAS) and informed me that there was now a second edition of the book prepared; he advised me to await it so that I could incorporate the updates and revisions it contained – not a large task, he assured me – just a matter of translating the extra chapter (chapter five) that had been added as a postscript.

The second edition was dated 21 March 1996, though I received it some months later. Unfortunately this edition, *actualizada* and *ampliada*, arrived not in a printed version but as a duplicated typescript that has not yet been published in Cuba. This, together with the fact the first edition is now out of print, makes it even more important to publish and distribute the English edition. The volume as presented here contains not only the authors' analysis of existing and proposed economic reforms designed to reorient the Cuban economy into the next century by transforming it into an efficient and cost-effective economy guided by socialist goals of equitable distribution of income, equality of opportunity and access to services and employment for all its citizens. It also contains an astute review of the literature – both Cuban and external – on socialist transformation and economic restructuring. In addition, the second edition contains updated statistical data on output, the balance of payments, the fiscal deficit, taxation policy, the monetary overhang, the legislation on self (own-account) employment, foreign investment and enterprise management.

The last chapter (i.e. the postscript written for the second edition) adds a detailed discussion on the authors' proposal for a progressive currency replacement as part of a monetary policy aimed at dealing with inflation, speculation, shortage of investment resources and the increasing income disparities caused by the opening of major sectors of the economy to 'market' forces.

There are some commentators who might see in these proposals a scheme to (re)instate a market economy in Cuba in which socialist objectives are reduced to maintaining state provisioning and delivery of health and education, which are agreed to be the cornerstone of the achievements of the Cuban revolution, a kind of social democratic welfare state built on the human resource development of the past decades of Cuban socialist history. But such commentators would in my view miss the point. What this volume seeks to do is to place the problematic of Cuba's restructuring within the real world of blocked international credit and aid, political conflict, external and internal disequilibria and an ageing population increasingly reliant on transfer payments whose real value is falling. Carranza and his co-authors have sought to address not only the objectives of socialist transformation, developing the forces of production and output and productivity of domestic resources, but also the *sustainability* of such a project in the current international context of adverse terms of trade, a volatile international political situation and the slow transformation of economic and other institutions developed to operate under quite different conditions in the first thirty years of the Cuban Revolution. Specifically, they stress that the raft of measures discussed and proposed in the book are conceived within the context of the continuation of revolutionary principles which include control of income disparities and the limitation of private ownership of property and resources compatible with opening new spaces in the economy for the operation of market-determined allocation of resources and output.

Particular elements of the restructuring model proposed in this volume include:

(i) a monetary policy aimed at minimising income differentials whilst freeing resources to develop in the context of transformed relations of production and employment;

(ii) a range of different relations of production in agriculture, industry and services (excluding education and health) aimed at incorporating new technology and maximising efficiency in different sectors;

(iii) the attraction of foreign investment across a wide spectrum of economic sectors in joint ventures with state-owned enterprises, which will be devolved to autonomous management and finance strategies;

(iv) regulation (including operating permits, taxation, health and safety conditions and employment relations) of self-employment, family-based business and small enterprises within a socialist-managed industrial structure;

(v) mechanisms of social and political control of evolving forms of enterprise which could ensure that new productive structures maintain socialist goals of productivity, relations of production and remuneration;

(vi) mechanisms to maximise foreign exchange earnings (and import-substituting foreign exchange savings). Although balance in the external sector is a central objective of a restructured Cuban economy, the authors stress that recuperation of the economy is based on domestic policies and the domestic economy which will facilitate a socially responsible adjustment;

(vii) the absolute importance of a bold monetary policy which will address excess liquidity and inflation in the domestic economy as well as channel investment capital accumulated by the regulated private sector *via* a financial market into socially approved investment in various sectors of the economy.

The authors challenge what they call the 'neo-liberal myth' that state/public enterprises cannot be profitable and efficient, arguing that within the context of a socialist-managed state, incentives and mechanisms for maximising efficiency are not only feasible but achievable.

As Luis Gutiérrez Urdaneta, another of the book's authors, stressed to me at a conference in Canada in November 1996, this represents a proposal for a debate rather than any specific blueprint for future policy. Indeed, many readers will require more information about the proposals to instal 'internal markets' within state-owned decentralised enterprises, and require demonstration of the claims that the enterprises run by the present armed forces constitute the model for the efficient management of decentralised enterprise in socialist Cuba in the future. Likewise, much trust and little evidence is presented in the efficacy of measures to improve the output of the agricultural sector, which up to the end of 1995 was still running at a fraction of the levels of the 1980s.[2] The combination of decentralisation of state enterprises, incentives to individual and cooperative producers and the encouragement of selling specified surpluses in the agricultural markets have begun to cut the levels of food imports; however, the much heralded import-saving techniques of low input organic production are reported to have receded in the face of chronic labour shortages, an increase in access to imported fuel and chemical inputs and the pressures on producers to increase output in the short term.

The measures proposed for regulation and control of private enterprises – both own-account businesses and larger firms employing wage labour in local committees of *Poder Popular* – appear to ignore the fact that the entrepreneurs are part of the local communities and thus part of the participatory structures set up to regulate them. The ways in which such enterprises have to be regulated and accountable to state and community would seem to require a further development of policy and legislation beyond the initial discussion in this volume.

The authors' elaborate arguments in favour of a progressive and confiscatory currency substitution are persuasive, given the objectives of reducing income differentiation and channelling accumulated surpluses into productive investment. However, in the light of the rejection by the Cuban government of a currency substitution – whether for reasons of practicality, fear of capital flight and loss of confidence by foreign investors, risk of political unpopularity or the new conditions induced by the passage of the Helms Burton Law through the US Congress – one might argue that there is a need for a third edition to extend the debate on monetary policy for a socialist transformation in Cuba.

The future of Cuba's economic policy has attracted a wide range of commentators both external and in Cuba, offering a range of 'solutions' tempered both by their political and their intellectual position as well as their familiarity (or otherwise) with the concrete conditions prevailing in Cuba today. The authors, address both theoretically, and analytically the challenge facing Cuba: the construction of socialism in terms of relative scarcity in a post-Cold War world. They go beyond rhetorical appeals to socialist human nature or the

---

[2] See Armando H. Portela, 'Agriculture, Nowhere to go but up', *Cuba News*, October 1996, p. 11.

'new man' seriously to examine the appropriate balance in such an economy between the market and the central planning mechanism, as well as addressing the processes whereby such a balance could be constructed and maintained.

The purpose of translating and disseminating this book in English is to contribute to this project by exposing the analysis it contains to a wider audience of economists and analysts. Cuba has certainly taken significant steps to adapt to the harsh realities of the 1990s. The continuation of a socialist transformation will require all the creativity of socialist economic planners and analysts, and the 'contribution to the debate' represented by this book is central to the dialectical methodology of socialist analysis.

Ruth Pearson
School of Development Studies, University of East Anglia and Institute for Social Studies, The Hague, Netherlands

February 1997

Preface

This is the second – updated and expanded – edition of the text of the book published in 1995 by the Editorial de Ciencias Sociales del Instituto Cubano del Libro, in Havana.

Like the first edition, this new material has been constantly threatened by the danger of becoming out of date, at least as far as the descriptive elements and some of the proposals, although we think that its central objective – the presentation of an integrated programme for economic restructuring – has not been affected by the passage of time.

The preparation of the text has coincided with one of the most intense periods of transformation of Cuba's political economy in recent years, in which many changes have taken place – often very quickly and quite unpredictably – that more than once have changed the starting point for the economic programme that we are trying to articulate. In the event, some of these changes coincided with measures included in this analysis. We have not suppressed in this edition all the proposed elements of restructuring contained in the text of the original project, in order to convey to the reader the integrated 'architecture' of the programme. In fact, some of the most recent changes coincide with measures contained in our original proposal, and these have been incorporated as footnotes.

Under these conditions we run the risk of writing history, a laudable activity but not the aim of this present work. So we have tried to meet the challenge imposed by the chronological separation of parts of the analysis as 'grace under pressure', which has to be lived through in exceptional times like the present.

This book is, in essence, the development of an earlier and less comprehensive analysis, predominantly a policy proposal, which was presented to the government in April 1994. Subsequent to that the authors embarked on an expansion and major revision of the original text, which has resulted in a new version containing a more rigorous conceptualisation, updated by the incorporation of the events of May–August 1994. We then updated the text to January 1995, for the first edition of the book.

The new version of the book, which has been prepared for this second edition, not only incorporates the most significant updates required by the passage of time, but also includes expansion and modification of some of the original sections. In particular, because of the importance of the topic, we decided to include as a postscript an article written by the authors in January 1996 entitled 'The demonetisation of the Cuban economy: a revision of the alternatives'.

In deciding to bring out a second edition there were at least two important factors. First, the pressure of interest from people within and outside Cuba who were unable to obtain copies of the text because of the limited print-run of the first edition; and secondly the importance that the authors believed should be given to the preparation of new materials that would allow the original book better to meet the exigencies of a debate which, given its connection with reality, is essentially characterised by change.

As with the first edition, this book has benefited from the constructive and critical comments of various colleagues too numerous to mention here. For the preparation of the second edition we were able to receive comments from a wider group of readers from a range of backgrounds and from the most diverse professions and occupations, who stimulated us to continue working on our ideas; in particular we benefited from the exchange of ideas with the general public which has offered us important insights from the particular perspective of ordinary people – sometimes called popular knowledge or common sense – offering useful reflections on economic issues such as are often not found among specialists.

During the time since the publication of the first edition, the dissemination of its contents has benefited from the interest and support of diverse bodies such as the Cuban press, academic institutions, government bodies and the National Association of Cuban Economists.

The authors are aware that in the interval between writing these notes and the publication of the book, time and, more significantly, the speed of change will have overtaken us once again. However, we think that the fundamental objective of our project will have been achieved to the extent that we have provided material for one of the most important debates in Cuba at the present time.

The authors: Havana, March 1996

Introduction

This book was stimulated by a range of objectives, the most important being the need to focus our analysis to respond to the challenges faced by the Cuban Revolution at the present time.

The implications of the discussion of the Cuban question reach beyond the borders of the country. Like it or not, this is also part of an overarching debate about socialism and possible alternatives for the left. In fact this is a flourishing and wide-ranging debate, shaped by the ways in which the historical conjuncture presents different perspectives for socialist alternatives: from the optimism of the October Revolution, the end of the Second World War and the revolutions in the Third World to the pessimism generated by the final outcome of Perestroika and the socialist experience of Eastern Europe.

Without ignoring the fact that inevitably our own discussion will be affected by this global debate, we have concentrated on the specific experience of Cuba – particularly on the complicated situation in which the country has found itself since 1990. In our view this debate is provoked less by the theoretical debate about socialism and the experience of 'actual socialisms' than by the concrete (geo-)economic and (geo-)political conditions within Cuba.

The strong integration of the Cuban economy within the Council for Mutual Economic Assistance bloc of countries (COMECON – or CAME in Spanish) was not due just to ideological compatibility, but also to the fact that this was the sole alternative to the blockade which US governments imposed on Cuba since the earliest years of the Revolution. This integration, although it was not without tensions and contradictions, generated progressively over nearly three decades a model of economic relations that to a large extent allowed us to escape the difficult conditions imposed on underdeveloped countries by the world market. A range of measures, including preferential prices, development credit, settlement of commercial debts, and technical and military assistance, provided the national economy with sufficient resources to sustain a high level of investment and an expanding level of social expenditure.

The Cuban economy was organised according to the principles of central planning – albeit with substantial differences between the 1960s and the decades of the 1970s and 80s – leaving a very restricted role for monetary and market relations, perhaps less than was objectively sustainable even under the then favourable conditions of Cuba's international economic relations.

From 1990 there was an abrupt change in the international links between Cuba and its international trading partners. Cuba was exposed directly to the world market, the US blockade was strengthened – now reinforced by the Torricelli Law (1992) – and the persistent problems of economic efficiency that had not yet been resolved became more conspicuous and costly. This is the immediate cause of the current crisis in the economy, and the debate about what to do and how to do it must be guided by these circumstances.

This is not an abstract discussion on the viability of socialism, nor a debate amongst factions of the left who like to discuss what policies they might follow if they ever achieved power. Nor are we dealing with a country that is well endowed with natural resources or that is not in a situation of international conflict, which might seek a route to re-articulate within the contemporary world economy. The basic problem is to restore the economic viability of a small, poor and besieged economy. Not economic viability on any terms, but terms that, along with economic growth, will enable social justice and national independence to be sustained. And this must be done here and now.

Our view, therefore, is that the Cuban economy requires a profound restructuring which will include the redefinition of the bases for accumulation, its reinsertion into the international economy and a reform of the economic system. But there is not just one single policy which can lead to such restructuring. We have to look at – and indeed we do look at – different paths of economic change, each one of which is largely determined by the kind of society we wish to construct. The viability of these proposals will be fundamentally determined by the extent to which they are based on a realistic assessment of the economic and political limits of the situation that we are trying to change.

In this book we are not discussing economic restructuring in general terms. We are, instead, focusing on what in our view could be a socialist and sustainable reform of the economic system,[1] given the concrete situation in Cuba. In other words, restructuring and economic reform are considered as equivalent terms in this context. We are trying to contribute to what we called in an earlier publication[2] an act of creation, which allows us to respond effectively to the challenges the Cuban Revolution is facing today.

This book is a contribution to discussion, in the sense that it contains proposals. On the one hand, as we explain in Chapter 2, it reviews controversial non-socialist economic plans proposed by various overseas authors and institutions. On the other hand, it is located within the internal debates about how to achieve the re-articulation of the economy and the socialist project in Cuba.

In our view the survival of socialism in Cuba necessitates a *fundamental economic restructuring* which will introduce significant changes in the basic

---

[1] The definition of economic system used in this book emphasises the configuration of institutions which define at least four fundamental aspects: (a) the mechanism of coordination (including decision-making, generation and transmission of information, and motivation of economic agents); (b) ownership; (c) feedback mechanisms from decisions; and (d) the nature of organisation and control of intra-firm relations.

[2] See Carranza Valdés (1992).

structures of the current economic system, without jettisoning its socialist principles. It is therefore necessary to set down some basic notes on the concepts of socialism and economic reform.

The disappearance of so-called 'real socialism' in the former Soviet Union and Eastern Europe represented a severe blow to this specific form of socialism. It became evident that 'real socialism' – also called classic socialism – was not sustainable in the long term. Therefore, the theoretical question of the viability of socialism has become, fundamentally, a problem of substantially redefining the concept. There is not a unique definition of socialism, but at least there is sufficient consensus that the notion of socialism implies a particular sort of ownership; that is, a system of ownership in which there is genuine social control of, and benefit from, the basic means of production.

Of course, a more complete definition of socialism would not be limited to the hegemony of social ownership and of planning, its logical corollary, but would extend to include democracy. From the existence of these basic aspects we can derive other characteristics such as social justice and the formation of a new consciousness of solidarity. However, we have highlighted social ownership and control of property here as the necessary condition of a socialist project. According to a well-known theorist, 'Without social ownership of the means of production, the term "socialism" loses its original meaning and is transformed into a general term which refers to a better society which can be interpreted in diverse ways. It indicates an alternative but does not define it'.[3]

Centrally planned economies have had to incorporate, almost as permanent features, a series of modifications to different aspects of the economic model. Sometimes many of these changes have been identified incorrectly as economic reforms when they are really processes of reorganisation of the methodology and administration of the planning system, rather than indicating any significant variation in the economic model.

In the context of a socialist economy we understand by reform not these kinds of changes in the system of planning and administration, but modifications in the principles which inform the system and which imply moving to new economic mechanisms.[4] Although socialist economic reforms have been of varied significance and intensity, including movements towards a higher degree of centralisation and state control, seen in perspective the most significant modifications of the principles of operation of socialist economies have consisted in a reduction in the role of the plan as a central instrument of resource allocation and coordination within the economy.

---

[3] Przeworski (1989).

[4] By the economic mechanisms of a classic socialist economy, we mean methods of planning and administration as well as relations between economic agents.

The history of socialist economic reform[5] demonstrates that radical changes such as the so-called 'New Economic Mechanisms' (NEM) in Hungary after 1968, or the current economic reforms in Vietnam,[6] have been the exception. The 'deepening' of the reforms in countries such as Hungary and Poland at the end of the 1980s represented an important challenge to the principles of centrally planned economies, but the political evolution of those countries placed such reforms within so called 'post-communist transitions' rather than within socialist reforms.

In the main, socialist economic reforms have been partial – i.e., limited or incomplete modifications of the principles of the economic mechanism. These partial reforms have been of two types: those designed for sectors or specific areas rather than the whole economy, and those implemented in an incomplete manner.

For example, the economic reforms initiated in the People's Republic of China from the end of the 1970s and the beginning of the 1980s in agriculture, the export sector, and later in industry, belong to the first type.[7] However, most commentators consider that the limited success of economic reforms in China, apart from their partial and contradictory nature, are due to their specific characteristics which are difficult to replicate in other socialist countries.[8]

The other kind of partial economic reform is characterised by its incomplete implementation, even when, as is often the case, its initial proposals were much more wide-reaching. Although in each case the partial nature of the reforms has a concrete explanation based on different factors, there has been an attempt to construct a general model which some writers have called 'the reform cycle' in which political factors have played a key role in the appearance of counter-reform tendencies.[9] Other writers characterise the majority of socialist economic reforms from the well known Soviet New Economic Policy (NEP) of the 1920s to those introduced in the former Soviet Union and Eastern Europe in the 1980s as partial reforms from the outset, a process identified as 'dynamic petrification'[10] in the sense that it dealt with minor adjustments which did not substantively modify the principles of the operation of the economic system.

---

[5]　Here we identify as socialist reforms the economic changes in various socialist countries at different historical moments, which were aimed at 'improving' socialism rather than replacing it with overtly capitalist economies, such as has occurred in East Europe since 1989.

[6]　The radical nature of some of these experiments has not necessarily guaranteed their success – for example, the NEM in Hungary.

[7]　The partial nature of the reforms initiated in China at the end of 1978 stems from their limited scope. However, we should acknowledge that there have been significant changes in the principles of the functioning of the economic sectors where reform was applied.

[8]　See Harrold (1992); Chen, Jefferson and Singh (1992); Tidrick and Jiyan (1987); Feinerman (1991).

[9]　See Brus (1985).

[10]　This term was coined by Wladyslaw Bienkowski in his book *Theory and Reality*, cited by Alex Nove in *The Economics of Feasible Socialism* (1983).

A critical theory has also developed in regard to socialist economic reforms, to the effect that the classic socialist system is incapable of renewing itself since partial modifications fracture its internal coherence. From this point of view, reforms are condemned to failure by the very nature of the system, which does not admit of 'improvements' because if these are applied in a sustained and coherent manner they unleash internal contradictions that may lead to so-called 'post-communist transitions'. This negative vision of socialist economic reform reflects a basic perception of the systemic non-viability of so-called classic socialism.[11]

The most serious criticism of this theoretical perspective is that it only addresses reforms aimed at maintaining the economic mechanism of classic socialism, based on a centralised planning system. However, another kind of socialist economic reform is possible – at least in theory – which we have called fundamental reform.[12] This consists of substantial modifications in the economic mechanisms to the extent that they represent a general and fundamental change in the socialist model: reforms which facilitate the movement from classic socialism to another form of socialism. We are not talking about changes which are carried out within a given model of socialism, but those which will construct the transition from one model of socialism to another. This transformation in our view necessitates granting an active role to the market,[13] although not an exclusive or dominant role, in the distribution of resources and in the general functioning of the economy. The market will play a much more important role than it has in the classic socialist model and in most socialist reforms to date.

A further consideration for planning an alternative socialist model is its relationship with any long term vision of society. Within traditional Marxism, socialism has been seen as the first stage of communism, which has had practical relevance for the construction of socialism in that it has been assumed – often quite unjustifiably – that the 'socialist stage' must demonstrate certain tendencies and characteristics of future communism, that is, attributes of the ideal. Therefore, certain socialist phenomena – such as the market – have often been judged in a negative manner because they are seen as 'alien', 'concessions', or 'deviations' from the communist ideal without sufficient analysis of their relevance as practical concrete processes. We will not digress here to discuss this issue, which is inevitably very polemical, but just note that to confuse the model of constructing socialism with the prefiguration of the future, to which it aspires in the long term, represents a major obstacle to the transformation of the present.

If socialism is to be viable, it has to be viable in conditions of relative

---

[11] See Kornai (1980); (1987); (1990); (1992).

[12] This type of reform is frequently referred to in the literature as 'radical reform'. The current reforms in Vietnam are an example of fundamental economic reforms.

[13] At this concrete level of analysis of the economy we understand by 'market' the economic process in which supply and demand are related in order to determine prices and volumes of goods and services.

scarcity as is the case with all production models, that is, in contexts where there is conflict over distribution of resources. Socialism does not eliminate 'the economic problem' of society, but offers a specific form of confronting this, distinct from that offered by capitalism. Thus, it must be acknowledged that the idealisation of the socialist economy is a negative factor in its functioning. Socialism must not assume 'immaculate' characteristics; conflicts of interest must be understood as a normal part of the functioning of the economy and not automatically as a regression to the past, or an imperfection or a conspiracy.[14] It has been a central assumption of this book that we have never considered that the economic restructuring we are proposing will be a process exempt from contradictions.

The classical socialist model attempted to resolve the problem of distribution of resources *via* an economic mechanism in which the role of central planning was almost absolute. However, it is not an exaggeration to say that the prime preoccupation of socialist economic theory is to determine appropriate principles and divisions of labour between planning and the market.

The development of a new socialist economic paradigm must start from the recognition of the inadequacy of the market, in capitalist economies, to ensure the efficient and rational distribution of resources. It is not our intention to list here what the economic literature has registered as 'market failures', nor to discuss the disparity between the hypothetical and actual functioning of capitalist markets. The partial irrelevance of the abstract assumptions of perfect competition in theories of general economic equilibrium makes untenable the notion of the market as the sole regulator of economic efficiency.

In fact, in spite of its contradictions, capitalism has been viable, precisely because it has not functioned solely on the basis of market regulation. The hegemony of the market is not in dispute, but the history of capitalist economics reveals the existence of an active role for the state in economic policy in order to correct and complement the action of the market, including the redistribution of income.[15]

The existence of 'degrees of substitution' between state policy and the market is a self-evident and well-documented characteristic of the capitalist economy. However, there are also a number of studies demonstrating how such 'degrees of substitution' have developed within classic socialism, and the noted divergence between the hypothetical and actual functioning of the principal mechanism of state intervention in such societies – the planning system.

The list of 'socialist planning failures' is also extensive and well-documented. There are many studies concerning the general failure of attempts to reconcile

---

[14]   See Brus (1985).
[15]   See Erber (1990).

planning and markets within classic socialist economies, an issue which has led some writers to assert that ' ... the possibility of effectively combining planning and market forces is an unjustified act of faith'.[16] However, the generally negative experience about the form in which such 'degrees of substitution' have been produced between planning and the market in socialist economies must not be taken as a criterion on which to base *a priori* the impossibility of combining both elements in a different model of socialist economies, where the relevant question is not only what is the optimal division between planning and markets, but the conceptual and practical acknowledgement of the active role of the market in the normal functioning of a socialist economy. The construction of socialism does not require the elimination of the market, but the suppression of the hegemony of capital, which is something different.

A socialist vision of the economy must always have reservations concerning the market, but should not underestimate it nor permit it a smaller role than that dictated by the concrete conditions in common-sense terms, and from the perspective of socialist theory cleansed of 'fundamentalism'. Often socialism has been thought of as the first post-market society, whereas in most cases it is the latest market society.

---

[16] See Devine (1988).

CHAPTER 1

The current situation

Several years ago an article was published called 'Cuba: the challenges of the economy', written by one of the authors of the present work,[17] in which there was an attempt to analyse and synthesise the current crisis in the Cuban economy.

Since that time the tendencies noted have accentuated, in spite of the relative improvement in the economy since 1994, and this has complicated the difficult circumstances in which the country's economy is located; at the same time a process of change in economic policy and in economic organisation in Cuba has been occurring. Some of these changes could in our view favour the restructuring of the economy, but others represent obstacles to the implementation of reform which we consider necessary to resolve our present problems. One of the most significant problems relating to these changes is that to date they cannot be seen as components of an explicitly formulated economic programme.

From the political point of view the most relevant factor is the capacity of management control which the government has retained throughout the five years of acute economic crisis and systematic hostility from the United States government, most clearly expressed in the intensification of the blockade.[18] The Cuban election results of February 1993 and other political events of that and the following year permit measurement of the level of consensus which the Revolution maintains, which is stronger than the relative loss of support found in distinct groups within the population.

Of course, the massive popular support for the government is not a vote of acquiescence in the crisis; rather it represents a recognition of the historical role of the Revolution in terms of Cuba's dignity and independence, social justice and progress, and also a demonstration of confidence in the capacity of the government to offer society a programme of changes and adjustments which will allow it to overcome the crisis and to re-articulate the viability of the Revolution within the new international conditions.

As we noted earlier, this is a complicated task, an act of creation, and we will have to follow a path that has no historical precedent, to restore economic efficiency and growth, reinsert the country into the world market without jeopardising the social achievements of the Revolution, and maintain national

---

[17]   See Carranza Valdés (1992).

[18]   In 1992 the 'Torricelli Law' was approved and in March 1996 the 'Helms-Burton Law' was also passed, both with the objective of internationalising and intensifying the blockade in order to strangle the Cuban economy.

independence. All this within a small island, poor in natural resources, without strong international allies, and in a difficult geographical position.

The Economic Scenario

1993 was the fourth consecutive year of negative growth in Cuba. The accumulated fall in Gross Domestic Product (GDP) between 1989-93 was more than 35%.[19] In 1994 the fall levelled off and in 1995 there was a recovery of 2.5% of GDP followed by further growth in 1996 [estimated at 7.2% – editor]. The reversal of the trends observed in the 1990-93 period has been very important, but conditions do not yet exist to guarantee the sustained recovery of the Cuban economy. On the other hand, the re-articulation of economic growth makes even more urgent the discussion of the social and economic structures in which it takes place.

The External Sector

The import capacity of the economy has continued to shrink as a consequence of the deterioration in the country's terms of trade, the contraction in the supply of exports and the impossibility of obtaining sufficient international credit. In 1994 only US$1,956 million of imports could be obtained. In 1995 there was a slight improvement in the economy's capacity to import, with a total figure of US$2,087 million, still well below the 1989 figure of US$8,139 million.[20] An aggravating factor in recent years has been the decline in the sugar harvest from 7 million tons in 1991-92 to 4.2 million tons in 1992-93, 4 million in 1993-94 and only 3.3 million tons in 1994-95. The implications of this are severe given the importance of sugar both in national output and in foreign exchange earnings.

The decline in the sugar harvest resulted from various factors, ranging from the historical levels of efficiency in the industry[21] to the conjunctural effects of the current crisis (lack of fertilisers, herbicides, spare parts and fuel). In addition, Cuba experienced adverse climatic conditions as well as serious organisational problems and a high degree of agro-technical negligence. The recovery of sugar production is essential for the future of the Cuban economy. In 1995 pre-finance schemes were established amounting to approximately 300 million dollars with the aim of guaranteeing higher levels of inputs which will permit a gradual recovery in this sector. The conditions established for foreign enterprises involved in these schemes were tough in terms of interest rates and repayment periods, which makes it all the more important to see rapid increases in production. This seems to be happening, as the 1996 harvest was

---

[19] For more comprehensive statistical information, see *Informe Económico*, Banco Nacional de Cuba (August 1995).

[20] See Fidel Castro Ruiz, 'Speech of 26 July 1993', *Granma*, Havana, 28 July 1993.

[21] See Alvarez Dozáguez (1993).

approximately 4.5 million tons.

Output of nickel, which is the second most important traditional export from Cuba, has been strongly affected by the crisis. Recent investment to modernise the three existing factories and the near completion of a fourth have been important factors in the recovery of the industry which also functions as the 'engine' of key supply for Cuba's metal-mechanical industry.[22] The prospects for the nickel industry began to improve after June 1994 when an important agreement was signed with a Canadian firm which could represent a very positive factor in the reactivation and sustained development of this key sector. After 1994, production of nickel began to rise and in 1995 it reached 43.2 million tons, approximately the same level obtained before the crisis. However, in the short term the fall in international prices has not translated this recovery into substantial increases in foreign exchange earnings.

Another export sector in the process of recovery is tobacco, which in 1994 and 1995 registered higher levels of production and exports. In 1995 it produced 553,000 *quintales*, 52% more than the previous year. Three factors have been important in the recovery of this sector. First, the distribution of 800 *caballerías* of land to private producers (up to November 1994), following Resolution 357-93 issued by the Ministry of Agriculture, and also the distribution for cultivation to private individuals of land which had previously been used to grow tobacco and which had in recent years been uncultivated.[23] Secondly, the agreement between *Cubatabaco* and *Tabacalera Española* that included the financing of 50% of the Spanish firm's tobacco import requirements by supplying, over three years, agricultural machinery, fuel, fertilisers, pesticides and other inputs required by the Cuban company, will allow Cuban production to stabilise.[24] Finally, *Cubatabaco* has embarked on an active campaign to promote international sales which has extended its own and other distribution channels to promote sales of tobacco products, particularly in Europe.[25] In September 1994 there was a substantial reorganisation of international marketing of Cuban tobacco with the creation of a new firm *Habanos SA* which replaced *Cubatabaco* in all export markets except France.

Citrus production, another important export product, has not achieved the levels of exports reached during the 1980s. This sector is also in the middle of

---

[22] See Eloy Concepción, 'Arrancan las "locomotoras"', *Trabajadores* (Havana), 13 June 1994; Rebeca Antúnez, 'A polvo rojo buena cara', *Trabajadores*, 20 June 1994.

[23] A partial survey carried out in Pinar del Río showed that the new producers had achieved on average higher outputs than the national average. See Raisa Pagés, 'Entregadas a familias más de 800 caballerías para cultivar tabaco', *Granma,* 22 July 1994.

[24] During the 1995 harvest 1,630 *caballerías* of land in the province of Pinar del Río benefited from the agreement between *Cubatabaco* and *Tabacalera Española*, which represented over 60% of land growing tobacco in the province. See Manolo Rodríguez Salas, 'Inician proceso de acopio y beneficio del tabaco', *Granma*, 28 May 1994.

[25] See 'Incremento de la producción y renta de habanos', *Business Tips on Cuba*, April 1994.

a radical restructuring including the modification of the production and export structure, based on an increase in processing and packaging capacity. Also, the plantations have been reorganised, key firms have introduced a self-financing system, and the fields have been tended by the Youth Work Army.[26] Agreements have also been established with enterprises in Chile, Israel and Greece which contributed to the recovery of citrus production in 1995 by 7% over the previous year.[27]

The remaining export sectors, apart from tourism, have not seen significant growth and have not improved their situation *vis-à-vis* international markets.

Tourism is the sector which has maintained the most stable growth levels during the crisis. In 1995 its gross income was 1,000 million dollars, more than 200 million higher than in 1994. The net income is estimated at 30% of the figures quoted. Part of this income belongs to foreign capital, given its high level of activity in this sector.

Import substitution has been most successful in the petroleum sector, with national output rising from 882,139 tons in 1992 to 1.4 million tons in 1995.[28] However, the high density and sulphur content of national crude continued to generate problems for its industrial use in spite of the advanced technolo:y utilised. Total consumption of fuel was 7.2 million tons in 1994, 6% higher than in 1993. These supplies were insufficient to meet the energy requirements of the country for production and domestic consumption. A problem which continues to affect the economic situation is the low energy efficiency coefficient. In 1994 a growth of 0.7% in GDP corresponded to a 6% growth in fuel consumption.[29] Import of foodstuffs and fuel represented 60% of total imports in 1995, compared to less than 40% in 1989.

During 1993, 1994 and 1995 there were attempts to get round the blocking of international credit by seeking alternative funds to pay the national debt. The alternatives were to sell exports or national assets; for example, Cuba re-negotiated its debt repayments with Mexico in exchange for investment in cement, communications and oil refining, and managed to liquidate the accumulated debt with this country.[30]

In 1993 Russia granted a 350,000 dollars credit, mainly to complete construction work started in the Soviet era, plus another credit of 30 million dollars to maintain the unfinished nuclear power plant at Juragua.[31] But the

---

[26] The Youth Work Army (EJT) is comprised of military units dedicated to production, especially agriculture.

[27] See *Informe Económico*, Banco Nacional de Cuba, August 1995.

[28] *Ibid.*

[29] CONAS (1996).

[30] Notimex, Cable 20 Sept. 1994.

[31] Interview with Lionel Soto in *Granma Internacional*, 29 Sept. 1993.

blocking of access to international credit continues to be an acute problem for the Cuban economy, and the debt continues to accumulate because of unpaid interest.[32] At the beginning of 1996, the external debt estimated in convertible currencies had risen to 9,161.8 million dollars.[33]

However, in spite of some advances in obtaining credit and increasing export earnings, the external constraints remain severe. The recovery of the Cuban economy will take place in the medium term and depends on variables within the domestic economy, since we cannot anticipate a fundamental change in international markets.

If the petroleum exploration currently being carried out in partnership with foreign capital were to be successful, this could considerably change the situation: Cuba would immediately be creditworthy. However, this does not change the necessity to effect a change in the internal dynamic of the economy that will allow Cuba to capitalise effectively on the potential benefits. In such a scenario the fundamental point is not greater access to fuel or new sources of credit, but how to utilise efficiently a new pivotal sector in order to dynamise the economy as a whole.

The Problem of Investment

The large decrease in production since 1990 initiated a process of de-capitalisation in the Cuban economy, as a result of the forced paralysis of substantial parts of national industry.

During the period of the crisis, investment has been concentrated in strategic sectors: (a) traditional export sectors (sugar, nickel etc); (b) non-traditional export sectors (tourism, medical/biotechnology productions, electronics-based medical equipment); (c) import-substituting sectors (food and fuel). Other sectors were relegated to a lower level of priority and, in effect, have not received the resources even to ensure their simple reproduction, much less for growth.

The maintenance of strategic sectors in the economy has to a large extent been achieved at the cost of decline or paralysis of others. However, the effect on production in those strategic sectors in which investment has been concentrated during recent years has been moderate. The fall in sugar production was the hardest shock for the economy in 1993, 1994 and 1995. Although food production grew slightly in 1995, it is still below the required levels.

Foreign investment has had to compensate for the deficiencies of the national

---

[32]   The recent positive experience of Cuba with the incorporation of *debt swaps* into negotiations with foreign investors, especially the Mexicans, indicate that this mechanism could be extended to overcome the present *impasse* in the Cuban debt situation.

[33]   *Informe Económico*, Banco Nacional de Cuba, August 1995.

economy, in order to allow for its reproduction. By the end of 1995, the amount of foreign investment reached US$ 2,000 million, although this was not sufficient to cover the deficit generated by the crisis. Moreover, there remains the danger that the growth in foreign investment beyond certain limits will become a major obstacle to the control of the country's basic resources.

High technology products (drugs, medical equipment and patents) seem to have achieved a relatively sustained level of growth, although this sector accounts for a very small proportion of national output – only 5% in 1993.[34] It is unlikely that in the immediate future these products will become a central and stable part of the national economy. The process of penetrating markets already highly internationalised, such as drugs, is slow, complicated and costly.

The strategic importance of the development of these products lies in the fact that they have a growing market in the world economy, and could play a key role in the future of the country, because of their capacity to exploit Cuba's key resource – the high skill levels of its labour force.

However, we must be careful to maintain a proper balance between the investment of resources in high technology sectors and the need to maintain traditional sectors such as sugar and nickel, given that a strategically better future depends in the first place on our ability to ensure at the present the reproduction of all the sectors of the economy.

As we noted earlier, tourism is the sector which has maintained the most stable levels of growth, albeit with the contradictions that accompany high levels of foreign involvement[35] and the level of imports it has generated.

From this examination of the present conditions and the international context in which the investment process has proceeded in Cuba, it is clear that there is a need for a restructuring of the domestic economy in order to achieve a higher return on investment through an increase in the productivity and intensity of labour.

Internal financial disequilibria

Since the beginning of the most acute phase of the crisis, in 1990, the Cuban government has tried to respond by means of policies which permit an equitable distribution of the difficulties and shortages imposed by the decline in the economy. This has implied policies which would both maintain the principal

---

[34] Statement by Ricardo Cabrisas, Cuban Minister of Foreign Trade, *Opciones,* 30 Oct. 1994 – 5 Nov. 1994, pp. 8-9.
[35] Up to October 1994 there were 27 agreements with foreign capital in the tourist sector (16.4% of all existing agreements). In addition, 37 hotel administration agreements were signed with foreign companies.

social gains (health, education and social security) and would not lead to unemployment nor to rises in official prices.

Therefore, a generalised system of rationing was imposed to ensure the equitable distribution of the limited supply of resources available to all social groups – prices would not rise in response to the fall in supply, but the limited supply of products and services would be shared equitably among the population as a whole at subsidised prices. Many enterprises which were affected by lack of assured supplies were kept open, in order to avoid an increase in unemployment; they continued to function on the basis of subsidies. The situation was made even more tense since the economy needed to incorporate an additional 300,000 people reaching working age between 1991 and 1995.

This policy of distributing the costs of the crisis to the population in a relatively equitable manner – which was important to retain the consent of the population in such difficult circumstances – has also generated a series of negative consequences which threaten the sustained economic reproduction of the country:

Excess money in circulation. The consequence of growth in demand (wages, social security, subsidies, etc.) in the face of a sustained fall in supply has been very serious. By the end of 1993 accumulated liquidity had reached 11,044 million pesos,[36] equivalent to more than 13 months' average wage payments. This implied a growth of over 50% in this indicator compared to 1989. In the conditions of contraction in demand, accumulated liquidity contributed to the high level of excess circulation.[37]

Budget deficit. The traditional sources of inflow to the national budget (profits from firms, circulation tax etc.) have been affected. In May 1994 69% of enterprises in the country were functioning at a loss and taxable products had a limited circulation.[38] However, in order to achieve the social objectives noted above, the state ran a deficit of 5,050 million pesos in 1993,[39] which represented a 90% increase over 1989 figures.

Growth in the informal market. The lack of supplies within the state trading system generated a rapid growth in the informal market, both in terms of its legal or tolerated forms and its illegal forms. By mid-1993 the informal market had grown to seven times its 1993 size, in value terms. There were various sources of goods which sustained this market from the resale of articles

---

[36]   Interview with José Luis Rodríguez, Minister of Finance and Prices, *Granma,* 22 Nov. 1994.

[37]   No precise figures are available on excess money in circulation, but this is estimated to have been more than 7,000 million pesos by the end of 1993.

[38]   After June 1994 the production and sales of cigarettes was stabilised, and an increase in the prices of these goods was a central component of the measures to reduce liquidity taken by the Cuban government in mid-1994.

[39]   Interview with José Luis Rodríguez, Minister of Finance and Prices, *Granma,* 22 Nov. 1994.

distributed through the rationing system to embezzlement and misuse of resources. A factor of growing importance has been the sale in national currency of articles which come from dollar shops, and also the direct sale of dollars. The sustained depression in supplies within the state system forced major sectors of the population to engage with the informal market to obtain their basic basket of consumer goods, especially food. Up to mid-1994 this market was characterised by inflation.

Labour indiscipline. The disequilibria noted above have led to the displacement of the wage as the principal mechanism by which intensity and productivity of labour are sustained. Since mid-1994 the level of wages received by the population has been in excess of that necessary to obtain the basic level of rationed goods, but insufficient to cover price inflation within the informal market. This created pressure on part of the population to enter informal markets not only as buyers but also as sellers, since this was the only way in which they could obtain the income necessary to continue to purchase in these markets. This generated an upward spiral of speculation. It also intensified the separation of a growing part of the labour force and tended to convert into a permanent rupture what had been a temporary separation, since the acute financial disequilibrium was a major deterrent to remaining within the formal labour market. The application of the financial rationalisation programme and the opening of markets operating at free prices in the second half of 1994 began to modify the situation described above.

All this had a very negative impact on a workers' society, not only in economic terms but also in ideological terms given that the wage – the economic and social reason to work – ceased to be the fundamental route for obtaining individual and family well-being.

The growth of financial disequilibria in the national economy forced changes in Cuba's economic policies which would permit restitution in the internal financial balances. In June 1994 a raft of measures was introduced to increase the appropriation of money in circulation: increase in prices of non-essential consumer goods, elimination of some free goods and the imposition of a new taxation policy. By the end of June 1995 there was a fall of 24% in the money supply; at this date the estimated level of liquidity was 9,062 million pesos – still substantially higher than the estimated required level, which was 3,500 million pesos. The budget deficit had fallen to 775 million pesos.[40] These measures, which contributed to a reduction in excess money in circulation and increased budgetary income, diminished the financial deficit, but they were inadequate in that they did not transcend the monetary sphere, which is where the imbalances became evident but not where their fundamental cause is found.[41]

---

[40]   See 'Informe sobre el plan económico y social para 1996', *Granma*, 27 Dec. 1995.
[41]   We will return to the theme of financial imbalances at various points in this book because of their importance in the view of the authors. Chapter 5 is dedicated to this theme.

The development of a dual economy

The depth of the crisis has led to an escalating process of economic reform. However, this has not been the result of a global programme whose conditions, scope, limits and gradual introduction have been considered in a comprehensive *a priori* manner. The process of change has consisted of the following elements:

Progressive opening to foreign capital. The basis for this was Decree Law 50 of 1982, originally introduced only for exceptional application. Since the end of the 1980s, however, and especially since 1990, this alternative form of investment has been widely utilised as a more general instrument for obtaining the capital, technology and markets necessary for the re-articulation of the reproduction of the economy, affected by the crisis in European socialism and the strengthening of the US blockade.

This process has not been carried out in an uncontrolled manner. The Cuban government has evaluated and either approved or rejected each investment proposal according to criteria based on the requirements and advantages for the country. However, the significance of this factor in the national economy has increased in quantitative and qualitative terms.

Most foreign investment up to 1991 was essentially in tourism, but since then this has become feasible in all sectors of the economy, except for those of strategic importance and those reserved for development with national resources. In 1992 certain parts of strategic industries were also opened to foreign investment, such as commercialisation of biotechnology-based pharmaceutical products.

In 1993 the representation of foreign banks in Cuba was approved in order to extend the financial services infrastructure available to foreign capital operating within the country. More recently, at the end of October 1994, the Cuban government announced that no productive sector of the economy would be barred to foreign investment, and that even real estate and property, and parts of the domestic market aimed at import substitution, would be open to foreign capital.[42]

In 1995 the Cuban parliament approved a new law of foreign investment which makes possible 100% foreign participation, and extends the arena for foreign investment to all sectors of the economy except public health, education and areas connected with national defence. The new law reaffirmed the principle of case by case approval by the government and of state control over the process of foreign investment.

---

[42] Speech by Carlos Lage, Secretary of the Council of Ministers and the Executive Committee in the inauguration of the XII Feria Internacional de La Habana, *Granma,* 1 Nov. 1994.

Growing presence of limited companies. These had almost disappeared as an institutional form from the Cuban economy. In the 1970s there were only 70 companies which operated abroad in order to facilitate international trade. These were regulated by article 66 of Law 1323 in 1976. In 1979 CIMEX was created, the first Cuban limited company operating within the country.

Since the end of the 1980s and particularly in the 1990s we have seen a growth in the presence of limited companies in the Cuban economy, as a consequence of the growth of joint ventures with foreign capital. By 1995 there were about 200 such companies, most of them within the country. The companies partly belong to joint companies (*Empresas Mixtas*) of Cuban and foreign capital; there were also some 40 limited companies owned by state capital which had adopted this institutional form to facilitate their international trade operations.[43]

Ending of the state monopoly of foreign trade. Foreign trade, which had previously been totally controlled by the Ministry of Foreign Trade (MINCEX) and to a great extent carried out by ministry enterprises,[44] has passed to the control of a growing number of enterprises (belonging to state organisations, and trading companies belonging to Cuban, mixed and foreign capital).

Self-financing of foreign exchange. More than 23% of existing enterprises have authorisation for self-financing in foreign currency in exchange for handing over part of their income to the national treasury. There are 30 different self-financing schemes of which one of the most comprehensive is that linked to the entity which acts as a finance house for the tourist industry, FINTUR.

Changes in the organisational structure of the state. Some of the organisational structures and functions of the state have been modified to meet the requirement of the new regime of foreign investment and joint ventures. The new Ministry of Foreign Investment and Economic Cooperation has developed direct links with foreign investors as part of its role within the state apparatus.[45]

Changes in the legal system. The most important change in this area was the Constitutional Reform of July 1992.[46] In economic terms its most relevant

---

[43] Declaration of Ricardo Cabrisas (see footnote 34).

[44] For many years, various foreign trade enterprises have been under the control of different units of the central state administration and not MINCEX.

[45] This point only refers to the changes in the organisation of the state directly linked to the institutional changes in the so called 'emerging economy', that is, basically, the Cuban export sector. Other organisational changes have also been adopted in recent times which, though not linked to this point, have been very important, in particular the reorganisation of the Cuban state apparatus in April 1994 on the basis of Decree Law 147. This established the restructuring of the Central Administration of the state, which since this date has consisted of 27 ministries and 5 institutes.

[46] The constitutional reforms agreed by the National Assembly of *Poder Popular* between 10 and 12 July 1992 comprised the incorporation of three new chapters, so that there are now a total of 15 in Cuba. The total number of articles was reduced from 141 to 137 and 77 of those were partly or

modifications are the redefinition of the rule of socialist ownership, the recognition of an emerging new form of ownership, the definition of other forms of ownership and changes in the economic planning system.

A well-known Cuban lawyer has summarised these changes thus:

> 'a limitation on the extent of socialist ownership was introduced which confined it to *fundamental* means of production. In the earlier constitutional formulation this underlined term did not appear, so that the concept of socialist ownership included the whole range of goods excluded from the other four forms of ownership recognised by the Constitution. The new specification opens the legal possibility of a redefinition of the scope of socialist ownership and, consequently, the acknowledgement of private ownership of many of these activities.
>
> In accordance with article 14, the modified article 15 transcends the irreversible character which characterised the socialist sector and expressly authorises the Council of Ministers or its Executive Committee to transmit goods from this sector to natural or juridical persons in the service of the economic or social development of the country. This formulation allowed for an amplification in the dispositions of Decree Law 50 of 1982 on the formation of joint ventures because 1) it does not distinguish as to the nationality of the acquirer, 2) it authorises acquisitions by personal title, 3) it opens the possibility of transferring full ownership, 4) it also leaves open the possibility of transferring other rights which up to the present time have been proscribed by law, particularly about assessments and real guarantees *via* contracted obligations.
>
> The new form of ownership emerging from the dispositions contained in articles 14 and 15 is added to the five which existed previously, *via* the specific acknowledgement in article 23 at least with respect to 'joint ventures, economic societies and associations that are constituted in accordance with the law'. The use, enjoyment and disposal of the goods of these enterprises are governed by what is established in the law, treaties, statutes and the regulations which govern them. The other four forms of ownership recognised in the Constitution retain their essential aspects – that is, property of small agriculturalists, agrarian cooperatives, personal property and the social and mass organisations.
>
> In its new formulation article 16 replaces the concept of the Unitary Plan of Economic and Social Development with 'a plan which will ensure the programmed development of the country'. It is obvious what is eliminated by this amendment, though not what is put in its place. If we take into

---

totally revised. See Azcuy (1992).

account that the Unitary Plan assumed an integral system which included foreseeing all the moments, phases, resources and links of the economy at the level of the basic units of the system, it becomes clear that this is precisely what is disappearing. The admission of private investment, and the consequent independence of its operations with respect to the state planning system and, even more, the necessity to allow a greater autonomy for state firms in the new conditions which will arise, imply that even though we will maintain the strategic objectives of socialist planning, its character is being transformed, with the substitution of part of its functions by a greater freedom of inter-enterprise commercial relations.'[47]

Another important change has been the reactivation of the Code of Commerce which establishes the legal framework for the functioning of private enterprise – Cuban owned or joint ventures. In 1992 the National Bank of Cuba approved Resolution 151 which regulates the operation of foreign exchange by different types of Cuban enterprises.

De-penalisation of dollar holding. Decree Law 140/93 legalised holding and trading in dollars in the whole of the national territory for all Cuban citizens. The growing availability of foreign exchange among part of the population stems from the growth of external factors in the social dynamic: tourists, foreign businessmen, Cubans resident abroad. The forms of transfer of foreign exchange are varied, including family remittances[48] and various payments to Cubans by foreign firms (gratuities, presents), as well as illegal transactions of some sectors of the population with tourists and businessmen.

Partial reform of prices and accounting systems. A reform of wholesale prices has been carried out in order to achieve a greater linkage with international prices, and a modification in the national system of accounting with the objective of making it simpler and more flexible, and compatible with international accounting practices.

These processes have allowed sectors of the economy to become more dynamic, to increase their earnings of foreign exchange and achieve a better articulation of the Cuban economy with international systems. But also, given that the process has been disjointed, this has provoked serious distortions in the internal functioning of the economy which compromise its strategic development.

In fact, the formal Cuban economy has a dual character today: the coexistence of two systems which have different organisational structures, actors and financial logic. On the one hand, there is the new or emerging sector where

---

[47]   *Ibid.*

[48]   As part of a raft of measures aimed at reinforcing the US economic blockade against Cuba, President Clinton announced on 20 August 1994 a ban on sending family remittances from the USA to Cuba.

joint ventures, limited companies or Cuban-owned companies and representatives of foreign firms predominate. Their fundamental activities are focused on exports or on domestic sectors that have foreign exchange (tourists, the companies themselves, the Cuban state or sectors of the national populations). The dollar is the currency which circulates in these sectors and it is influenced by market signals; it functions with prices of supply and demand and is not always subordinated to national priorities. This sector is characterised by a higher level of efficiency based on a superior level of material security and a higher recompense to its labour force.

On the other hand, there is the traditional sector of the economy, comprising the range of state enterprises which do not have transactions with foreign capital. Their fundamental orientation is the internal market and some key exports (consumer goods for the population, intermediate goods, non-export agriculture). This sector operates principally with national currency, is controlled by the mechanisms of central planning, has no control over its price levels and is subordinated to national priorities. It is characterised by relatively low levels of efficiency (with some specific exceptions) and its level of material security is unsatisfactory; its mechanisms of labour incentives have deteriorated as a result of the disequilibria and distortions which affect the whole economy.

The dual character of the present-day Cuban economy does not mean the existence of a modern sector and a backward sector inserted into the same economic dynamic, but of two sectors which are not strongly articulated and which have different financial, accounting, planning and legislative systems. The co-existence of these two sectors has increased the tensions in the internal economy expressed in phenomena such as the increase in the transfer of skilled labour from the traditional economy to the emergent economy. The free circulation of foreign exchange has increased these tensions. The informal market is open to two different circuits; one which operates with foreign exchange and the other where the same product has a price in national currency equivalent to its dollar price, which depends on the movement of the exchange rate within the informal market itself.

The analysis of the economy from this perspective reinforces the importance of a restructuring of the economy towards an integrated system which can recapture the necessary equilibria and move towards growth and development.

Recent Transformations in the Cuban Economy

Until mid-1993 the organisational and normative changes related to external aspects of the Cuban economy. However, from mid-1993 the government began to adopt measures which indicated the beginning of changes in internal economic policy. At the beginning of 1996 this process was still not fully developed and did not appear to form part of a wider and integrated programme of economic transformation.

However, what is most significant is that the measures taken since 1993 have gone beyond those concerning the orientation of trade in the external markets (foreign trade, tourism and foreign investment) and have begun to relate more directly to the cautious expansion of domestic markets.

In addition to the legalisation and the expansion of the circulation of foreign exchange, the two most important measures affecting the domestic economy in 1993 were (a) the establishment of a new legal regulation for own-account work, and (b) the introduction of organisational changes in agriculture in favour of cooperative forms of production, which can be considered as the first step in an important process of economic reform in Cuba.

Later, in 1994, new measures were adopted which extended the process of creation of internal markets, appropriate for the functioning of an economy with a greater range of economic actors. These measures were: the creation of the so-called farmers' markets; the approval of the functioning of industrial and handicraft markets from December 1994; the adoption of a new tax law; and the creation of new foreign exchange offices which operate at rates determined by supply and demand. The main characteristics of these measures were as follows:

New legal regulations for the exercise of own-account work. Decree Law 141/93 and Resolution No. 1 of the Committee for Work and Social Security-State Committee for Finance (CTESS-CEF), adopted in September 1993, regulate and extend the authorisation for carrying out own-account work. Prices for these services are established according to supply and demand conditions and in the currency agreed on by those involved in each transaction.

By mid-1994 this process appeared to have reached a level of stability after two periods of instability – the first at the end of 1993 as a consequence of the adoption of a series of restrictive measures,[49] and the second as a result of the application of Decree Law 149, particularly between May and August 1994.[50] By December 1994, 208,000 licences had been issued to own-account workers.

---

[49] The initial legislation (8 September 1993) defined 117 categories of activity which could be carried out as own-account work. In December 1993 the granting of new licences was suspended for five of these categories and permits in another category were revoked. At the same time strict regulations were adopted for those who held licences for preparation and sale of food. Later, new categories were incorporated which expanded the total range of activities which were authorised as own-account work. Also, precise regulations for these activities were established in each province and municipality. See 'Regulaciones especiales para el ejercicio del trabajo por cuenta propia en Ciudad de La Habana' established by the Provincial Administration Council, City of Havana, 12 December 1993. *Tribuna*, 12 Dec. 1993.

[50] Decree Law 149, issued on 4 May 1994, was adopted with the stated aim of confiscating 'goods and services obtained *via* unauthorised enrichment'. This was basically a process directed against people who had gained wealth by 'unauthorised means', mainly black market operators, known in popular Cuban slang as *macetas* (flower pots). See 'On confiscation of goods and services obtained via unauthorised enrichment', *Granma*, 5 May 1996.

Creation of the Basic Units of Cooperative Production (UBPC) from September 1993 and the establishment of the farmers' markets in October 1994. The creation of the UBPCs produced a fundamental change in the form of agricultural production, both sugar and non-sugar.

Up until October 1994, 93,800 *caballerías* of land, equivalent to 1,259,734 hectares, were incorporated in 1,221 UBPCs in the non-sugar sector. The average assets of these UBPCs were 800,000 pesos and they occupied 40% of the non-sugar state agrarian land. In coffee, UBPCs occupied 76% of the state-owned cultivated land in this product, and in miscellaneous crops (vegetables and horticulture) 69%; in rice 48%; in livestock 42%. UBPCs had the highest share of beef cattle – more than 68,000 *caballerías* (or 913,000 hectares). Some 600 UBPCs remain to be created in non-sugar production.[51] Up to July 1994, there were 1,555 sugar UBCPs which accounted for all the state sugar production – some 80% of total cultivation.[52]

The productivity of large state farms was affected by lack of fuel, fertilisers and spare parts, and also by general inadequacies of the national economy, and they were being replaced by smaller scale cooperative producers which had modified their incentive system. The producers associated with the UBPCs did not obtain legal ownership of the lands, but owned the output and, therefore, shared the profits. Until September 1994 the state was their only market and also was responsible for determining production quotas and fixing price levels which constrained the extent of direct legal sales from surplus production.

On 1 October 1994 the farmers' markets started to operate in Cuba; these were a new mechanism in which all agrarian producers could sell their produce at prices determined by supply and demand.[53] This was undoubtedly the boldest of the economic policies adopted in 1994 and one of its consequences during the first year of its operation was the overcoming of some of the problems of the UBPCs.

The experience of the UBPCs has not been homogeneous. Before the creation of the farmers' markets, 41% of the non-sugar UBPCs were anticipating profits of 30.6 million pesos for 1994, whilst the rest expected losses of 67.6 million pesos. In the sugar sector, of the total 1,555 UBPCs, some 1,082 were profitable according to the Ministry of Sugar (MINAZ), although in fact the UBPCs had not been able to reverse the decline in the agricultural phase of sugar production.[54]

---

[51]   Raisa Pagés, 'Incorporados a UBPC el 40 porciento del fondo de tierras no cañeras', *Granma,* 11 Nov. 1994.

[52]   *Boletín de Información Económica*, IPS, 30 Sept. 1994.

[53]   The farmers' market was established by Decree Law 191 of the Council of Ministers, issued on 19 September 1994. The other important legal instrument to make this market function was the *Resolución Conjunta* of the Ministries of Agriculture and Domestic Trade, 20 September 1994.

[54]   *Boletín de Información Económica*, IPS, 30 Sept. 1994.

In general, there has been a positive trend in the UBPCs towards an increase in productivity, better utilisation of the working day and available resources, and stricter cost controls. Some specialists argued that the UBPCs had received land already planted under the old system. However, an important group of UBPCs had serious problems with their initial start up. Combined with foreseeable problems such as lack of raw materials of all types (quality seeds, fertilisers, pesticides, fuel for irrigation and machinery, lack of spare parts), they also suffered from unprofitable use of resources, fluctuations in labour supply, bad utilisation of the working day and incompetence in administrative management.

During their first year the UBPCs complained of inadequate incentives and excessive interference from the state, and they demanded direct access to the market to sell surpluses, and priority in the sale of construction materials. One of their most intractable problems has been the impossibility of changing the mentality of those involved in the UBPCs – both producers and state officials. The latter would not readily give up the prerogatives and functions they had exercised under the previous administration, and the producers did not consider themselves owners of what they produced.[55] The farmers' markets can contribute a solution to these problems in that they enable the members of the UBPC to act as owners of their production, though changes in other spheres will also be necessary.

Creation of industrial and artisanal markets from 1 December 1994.[56] Various economic agents participated in these markets: so-called 'diverse local industries', enterprises linked to the central administration of the state and those linked to local government, and individual producers operating as own-account workers or otherwise authorised. The state-owned units were able to sell production in excess of that committed to fulfil the central government targets, and also unwanted stocks. The markets facilitated direct relations between buyers and sellers and prices were determined by supply and demand.

Adoption of a new taxation law. In mid-September 1994 Law No. 73 was adopted by the National Assembly which established new taxes and charges, and modifications in existing ones. Although the new tax law has been associated with the rationalisation of internal financial systems, its real importance lay in establishing a tax system designed to function in an economic system characterised by a plurality of economic agents. Thus, the tax system seemed to be in line with economic policy which was progressively oriented towards

---

[55] *Ibid* and Raisa Pagés, 'Radiografía de las UBPC de cultivos varios', *Granma*, 25 June 1994; 'Encuentro de UBPC habaneras', *Granma*, 2 July 1994; 'Irradiar los mejores ejemplos y combatir las ineficiencias', *Granma*, 16 July 1994; Sonia Castillo, 'Encuentro Nacional de UBPC: eficiencia por bajo costo y no por altos precios', *Juventud Rebelde*, 17 July 1994.

[56] These markets were established by Decree Law 192 of the Council of Ministers, issued on 21 October 1994. Among other important legal instruments for the establishment of these markets was the *Resolución Conjunta* of the Ministries of Domestic Commerce and Light Industry, 21 October 1994.

diversification in the economy and the development and functioning of markets.[57]

Establishment of foreign exchange offices. In the second half of 1995 the exchange offices enterprise (CADECA S.A.) began to operate with branches in various provinces. These carried out currency transactions (buying and selling of Cuban pesos). Currency transactions for personal requirements were legalised within the country at rates very different from the official exchange rate (one peso to one dollar) used for accounting and foreign trade purpose. The initial rate adopted by CADECA S.A. was linked to the black market rate, which later declined steadily.

These changes in economic policy are compatible with the economic restructuring that we consider Cuba needs. However, the adoption of these and other elements of the current economic policy – such as financial rationalisation – in a piecemeal fashion has caused problems in the implementation of these measures and could compromise their future success. By the beginning of 1996 it was clear that the tendencies towards market orientation of the economy and the recognition of diverse economic agents, initiated scarcely a year before, had been transformed into relatively stable elements of Cuba's current economic policy. However, this made it even more important to develop an integrated policy of economic transformation, in order to overcome the fragmented and uncoordinated manner in which the reforms were introduced.

---

[57]   A broader discussion on the importance of taxation appears in Chapter 5.

CHAPTER 2

Proposals from outside Cuba for Cuba's economic transition: paradigms and terms of the debate

As we noted above, the current economic situation in Cuba requires a complex process of transformation. The nature of the proposals for change is linked directly to the type of society to which we aspire, with the paradigms and the perceptions of the concrete situation that are entailed. This has led to a wide-ranging discussion, from non-socialist alternatives proposed from outside Cuba to an internal debate whose common element is the search for a re-articulation of the economy which will not betray the social gains of the Cuban socialist project.

In this chapter we examine briefly, and critically, some elements of the main suggestions emanating from abroad.[58] Although we must make it clear here that there is no intention of responding in depth to these proposals, which would be to go beyond the aims of this work, we consider it important to discuss them briefly in order to understand better the conceptual and practical elements which underlie the proposal we put forward later in this book as a socialist and viable alternative for Cuba.

Our criticism of these proposals – most of which are at a high technical level – is concentrated on two aspects: first, insufficient understanding of the Cuban reality, which leads to mistakes about the points of departure and incorrect estimations about the effectiveness of certain economic instruments; secondly, the ideological and conceptual premises of the proposals.

---

[58] In this analysis we have only considered a range of *academic* proposals, fundamentally from the USA, where proposals for economic transition in Cuba have been most widely discussed. We are not concerning ourselves with proposals directly connected with political organisation or with analysis from non-academic sources since, although these have purported to be recommendations or proposals, they have remained at the level of commentaries on the Cuban economy (for example, the well-known 'Report on a Visit to Havana' published by Jacques de Groote and Frank Mosse of the IMF at the end of 1993). Nor have we considered works such as the 'Informe Solchaga', since we were only able to obtain a copy of the article written by Carlos Solchaga, 'Cuba: Un informe integral de la reforma' (mimeo, Madrid, July 1994), after the first edition of our book had been finished. Also after completing the first edition, we were able to consult an article written by the same author, published in the journal *Actualidad Económica* (17 October 1994) under the title 'La transición cubana'. We were later able to communicate directly with Carlos Solchaga and to obtain documents prepared by him and his team of researchers. These works deserve a serious analysis which, for reasons of space and publishing pressure, we are unable to engage in at this moment. However, we wish to state that we have fundamental differences with important parts of the policies suggested by them, above all because they point to a different social paradigm than the one proposed in this book. To give one example, one of the main points of divergence concerns the limits and controls that must be imposed on the private sector, and the articulation of mechanisms of income distribution. Nevertheless, these documents contain one of the broadest and technically most rigorous programmes elaborated outside Cuba.

1991 marked the beginning of a new stage in so-called 'Cuban studies', characterised by the predominance of prescriptive types of study. The proposals for an economic 'transition' in Cuba have since then occupied a central place in academic and political analyses on Cuba carried out abroad. This intense prescriptive activity, however, contrasts with the virtual absence of such work published within Cuba.[59]

The design of economic plans in Cuba should not ignore studies carried out elsewhere, not because they contain key elements for the solution of our economic problems but because their critical analysis places in relief the necessity to develop a distinct conceptual base which will give internal coherence to the type of economic restructuring programme that, in our opinion, is most suited and practical for Cuba.

The conceptual basis and ideological orientation of most of these studies firmly identify their programmes as a transition to 'a market economy', or to be precise, to a capitalist economy.[60] Our own programme starts from different assumptions: it concerns a fundamental economic reform[61] which will produce significant transformations in the basic structures of the present economic situation without threatening its socialist essence.

The prescriptive type of studies that we have looked at can be classified into two groups: studies based on reforms in other countries and their possible lessons for Cuba, and explicit proposals for reforms in Cuba.

The proposals in the first group are implicit, loosely defined and above all based on other experiences of transition (see Annex I), whilst the studies in the second group present explicit proposals for the transition towards a capitalist economy in Cuba. Although most of these are of an integrated nature, there are also proposals for specific areas of transition[62](see Annex 2).

These proposals have been elaborated in a general context characterised by

---

[59]   The most significant of the possible exceptions to this is the work by Alfredo González entitled *Modelos económicos socialistas: escenarios para Cuba en los años noventa*, published by the INIE, Havana, May 1993. This work, although it is not in essence prescriptive, sets out a type of analysis which could be logically developed into a proposal.

[60]   The term 'market economy' is a common euphemism in the contemporary literature, used to refer to the capitalist economy.

[61]   We consider our own programme to be a fundamental economic reform because it would represent a step towards a new economic mechanism based on the creation of a regulated market for means of production and foreign exchange.

[62]   Within this group we have included the proposals developed by Manuel Pastor and Andrew Zimbalist. These authors refer to their work as having 'capitalist overtones'. However, in spite of our basic differences we acknowledge that this analysis differs from others in the second group and we do not address this work further in the present chapter. The work of Pastor and Zimbalist requires specific consideration which we are unable to give here because of pressure of space etc. In Chapter 5 we return briefly to their proposals, specifically to the proposal to consider privatisation as an element of macroeconomic stabilisation. See Pastor and Zimbalist (1995).

'stabilisation' and 'economic liberalisation' programmes in many countries, including a number in Latin America and the Caribbean; by the adoption by the former Soviet Union and Eastern European countries of transition programmes towards 'market economies'; and by the implementation of significant economic reforms in socialist countries such as China and Vietnam. However, in the case of the proposals on Cuba coming from outside, the significance of changes in the former socialist countries of Europe are very clear.

In the contemporary literature about economic transition there is a consensus about the specificity of the transition of socialist economies towards 'market economies'.[63] While these processes contain a component of 'stabilisation' sufficiently similar to other reforms – although there are differences as well – it is recognised that the construction of the market confers a very specific context to these transitions.

The identification of the principal characteristics of a programme of transition of a socialist economy to a market economy varies according to the writer, but a representative description of the main elements can be seen below:[64]

1. Macroeconomic stabilisation
2. Price and market reform
3. Enterprise reform
4. Institutional reform

These four main elements are shown in greater detail in Table 1.

In general, the proposals for Cuba's transition towards a 'market economy' emanating from the outside (see Annexes 1 and 2) are contained in the model described in Table 1, even though there are differences in the scale and degree of detail.

What turns these proposals into programmes for transition to a market economy is not their 'macroeconomic stabilisation' component so much as their structural reform elements – that is, the conjuncture of changes introduced with the object of eliminating existing restrictions on the functioning of the private sector.[65] The key aspects of the transition were massive substitution of social property by private property, the establishment of 'free markets' of factors of production, the opening of commerce, economic deregulation and the significant contraction of the economic role of the state; these, more than instruments or hypotheses, are assumed to be the only possible premises for the development of a dynamic and efficient economy.

---

[63]   See Fisher and Gelb (1991).

[64]   See Fisher and Gelb (1990), cited in Pérez-López (1993).

[65]   Authors such as Stanley Fischer identified these programmes of structural adjustment consisting in the combination of macroeconomic stabilisation with 'structural reforms' (policy and institutional changes). See Fischer (1993).

Table 1.

1. Macroeconomic stabilisation	2. Reform of prices and the market
– implementation of a stabilisation programme	– reform of internal prices
– creation of mechanisms and institutions of indirect macroeconomic control (fiscal and monetary control)	– liberalisation of foreign trade
– adjustment of fiscal and credit policies: • eliminate fiscal deficit • eliminate subsidies • establish a 'national anchor' to achieve price stabilisation • consider introduction of price and wage controls	– creation or strengthening of competitive factor markets: • promote measures to increase the flexibility of use of labour, relaxation of central regulation of wages, creation of unemployment payments and simulation of labour mobility • develop financial markets and private financial institutions, including banks
– control of excess money in circulation	
3. Enterprise reform	**4. Institutional reform**
– initiation of a process of restructuring: • create legal framework • introduce systems of company administration	– creation of legal and regulatory institutions: • legal framework for protection of property rights • commercial code (including the resolution of cases of bankrupcy) • rules for investment (including foreign investment) • taxation system
	– creation of social security system
– Initiation of a process of privatisation • define property rights • develop a methodology to determine prices of assets • develop a methodology to implement privatisation	– introduction of administration and control systems: • company administration • auditing and accounting • education and training

As we have noted above, criticism of these models for Cuba's transition to a market economy[66] can be developed on two levels: insufficient knowledge of the specific national reality, and the conceptual premises of the proposals themselves.

Inadequate knowledge of aspects of the Cuban reality gives rise to a series of assumptions which are highly questionable, if not irrelevant in terms of initial

---

[66] This refers to the proposals listed in Annexes 1 and 2.

conditions, levels of social and political tolerance, and the estimated effectiveness of the instruments and measures to be applied. It is interesting to note the importance that studies of reforms in other countries and their possible lessons for Cuba[67] give to 'political conditions and economic indicators' and the 'tolerance of the population', contrasted with the absence of an adequate evaluation of these factors in the models which propose explicit reforms for Cuba.

To cite a few examples, the starting point in Cuba does not correspond to the supposed 'totalitarian state ruled by a military dictator', 'poorly developed civil society', 'virtually shut off to current ideas in the world'.[68] Cuba today is, with all its contradictions, a much more complex and diverse society than that. On the other hand the social and political practice of its recent history and the development of ideology, values and egalitarian standards of conduct among wide sectors of the population do not correspond to the expectations contained in many of the programmes concerning the level of social acceptance of the transition programme.[69] Faced with measures such as wage freezes in a generalised context of freeing of prices, establishment of taxes and reduction of subsidies, all within a process of restitution of a capitalist economy which implies from the beginning a marked process of social differentiation, the Cuban working class will not react with the level of tolerance assumed in these models. On the contrary, open and active rejection will be the most probable reaction.

Lastly, the confidence placed in the immediate effectiveness of some instruments such as price rises, unrestricted commercial opening, the adoption of a single exchange rate, interest rates and the contraction of credit,[70] does not correspond – in spite of the note of caution introduced in some cases – with the real response which Cuban enterprises were able to give in the short and medium term. For these instruments to achieve a positive effect on the economic dynamics of firms, it is necessary first to develop more wide-ranging monetary mercantile systems and stricter financial controls in order gradually to alter the hitherto essentially administrative system of allocation of resources in the economy.

In the absence of a market and the almost total dominance of a state sector criss-crossed by distortions it is not possible to think in terms of the effectiveness of market mechanisms, which, introduced in one go, would disrupt the economy through the extremely inefficient allocation of resources that they would produce.[71] The correction of these distortions and the gradual construction of

---

[67] Particularly Jorge Pérez-López.
[68] Castañeda and Montalván (1993a).
[69] As Castañeda and Montalván assume, *op. cit.*
[70] *Ibid.*
[71] The authors do not see the market as a mechanism *per se* for the efficient allocation of resources. The point is that the intrinsic inefficiencies of the market will be made more extreme by distorted open economy.

a market economy are necessary conditions in Cuba's case to achieve the effectiveness of the economic instruments described above.

At this level the criticism made above will affect the implementation and effectiveness of these models. However, the fundamental criticism to make about these prescriptive works is that their basic premises – whether implicit or explicit – are not the only possible conditions for the development of an efficient and dynamic economy in Cuba.

These premises are those of a given model and cannot be considered universal. The attempt to consider certain assumptions as 'natural' is almost always an exercise in ideology. In the authors' view the actual probability of the introduction in Cuba of economic programmes such as those proposed in the models we have looked at is remote. But even if, hypothetically speaking, they were to be implemented – even in a different way from what is actually proposed, because of the problems we have already discussed – they are not the only possible economic model for Cuba.

The concept of the existence of alternative economic models is implicit in the science of political economy. This is the legacy of a science founded in debates between different explanations and prescriptions about the economic organisation of society. The fact that for the authors of this book the propositions noted above are not the preferred ones is not uniquely or fundamentally a question of ideological preference; it reveals, above all, the need to consider distinct theoretical premises in the analysis of economic problems.

In fact, the proposed transition of the Cuban economy towards a 'market economy' is part of a much wider series of changes in the economic paradigms and in the implementation of economic policy which has modified the terms of the contemporary debate on the conceptualisation of economic problems and the solution to them. The existence of a conceptual and discursive framework of a given type, and the generalised implementation of these concepts, not the intrinsic theoretical merit of their arguments, have been the fundamental factors in the dissemination and growing acceptance of 'neoclassical economic policy', whose influence extends even to those cases in which its 'purest' version has not been accepted.

There are various versions of proposals for Cuba's transition to a 'market economy' which are based on these conceptions. For example: the importance of static comparative advantage and the rejection of import substitution; the assumed contradiction between state intervention and export-led economic growth; the assumption that price distortions are less negative than distortions caused by government intervention and the assumption that distribution of resources by means of the market is always conducive to a competitive equilibrium. Within this paradigm everything which is not determined by the market is 'irrational'; everything which does not generate profits is 'inefficient'; and everything which inhibits the untrammelled functioning of factor markets is 'rigid'. In the non-economic sphere the promotion of individualism and the 'instrumental' treatment of people is elevated to the 'natural' state of affairs.

Without attempting to deal comprehensively with the elements of an alternative paradigm – such as socialism – in analysing the relative characteristics of the market, private ownership and the state, which are dealt with in the following chapter, it is important to clarify that in spite of the present crisis of credibility in socialist concepts the relative scarcity of socialist economic projects is more a reflection of a temporary act of resignation than an irreversible position of intellectual pessimism. All crises are disturbing and almost always affect the clarity of ideas, but given time ideas will settle again and mature. The critical analysis of proposals for Cuba's transition to a 'market economy' could be, under certain conditions, a stimulus for the necessary process of conceptual redefinition which will lead to the design of an alternative socialist economic model. That, for the authors of the present work, is the basic value of such proposals.

CHAPTER 3

Economic restructuring: conceptual considerations

As we noted in Chapter 1 the causes of the present economic situation in Cuba are many and complex. To overcome this a wide ranging programme of gradual economic change is required, to develop coherent actions in different areas over a relatively long timescale.

The planning of a programme to overcome the crisis and re-articulate development must take into account a series of conceptual elements, some related to the reproduction of an economy with the characteristics of the Cuban one, and others specifically associated with the programme of restructuring. On the other hand, some of these conceptual elements relate to general theoretical models, while others refer to concrete problems. But the relevant point is the need to understand certain basic concepts in order to design and implement practical measures.

In this chapter we do not attempt a detailed or complete analysis of the conceptual points relevant to the proposal for restructuring outlined later. The aim of this chapter is to note briefly some basic considerations which are necessary to understand the logical basis of our proposal.

We have divided our conceptual analysis into five sections in which we define concepts with different degrees of generality. We have tried, as much as possible, to relate our conceptualisation to the reality of the Cuban crisis and the proposed policies of economic restructuring.

Although this chapter is abstract by its nature, we have taken into account the premise that the programme of economic restructuring that is proposed has not been assumed by the authors to be a panacea for the present economic problems of Cuba but rather as a project which will, in the process of implementation, generate its own contradictions and could also lead to unforeseen effects. If the analysis in the following pages does not appear to give these problems the attention they deserve, this is not because of an involuntary lapse or an intentional omission, but rather because we prefer to concentrate more on the logic and 'architecture' of the programme and less on the prognosis of its evolution, which would require a separate analysis.

On the other hand, in the two following chapters we have tried to be concise in describing the positive aspects which we attribute to the components of the programme. In any case the essential 'virtue' that we perceive in the programme, and which we have repeatedly underlined, lies in its coherence and its integrated nature. However, at this point we must introduce two notes of caution: first, in no way do we consider this to be the only or the best possible model; and secondly, it will be the practice rather than the *a priori* criteria which will be the definitive proof of the 'virtues' of the programme.

Central Objectives and Sociopolitical Premises of Restructuring

In the first place it is necessary to define the central objectives of the proposed restructuring programme. These are:

– to recover the conditions for economic reproduction of the country;

– to reinstitute an internal economic dynamic, on the basis of a stimulus to individual and collective labour;

– to diversify and also reintegrate more logically the different sectors in the national economy in line with the present conditions of the economy and international markets;

– to preserve at the highest possible levels the socialisation of the economy and the social gains of the Revolution.

Thus, the proposed economic restructuring programme assumes a range of premises and conditions which must be preserved in order to guarantee its viability and its coherence with social and political objectives in the medium and long term. We have to begin from the principle of maintaining and reinforcing the fundamental gains of the Revolution. Therefore the socio-political premises have to be:

• To reproduce the political power of the people and the material conditions for its exercise in a more diverse economic context; to guarantee the socialised character of the economy under the direction of the state, the predominance of social forms of ownership (state and cooperative) and the preeminence of national interests.

• To strengthen representative and participatory democracy in order to guarantee the preservation and development of the interests of national development within the new national and international conditions, particularly on the basis of the activities of *Poder Popular* at all levels.[72]

• To strengthen the role of trade unions and other social organisations to defend workers' interests in the conflicts which could arise in the new situation. The workers will have a central role in determining working conditions and legislative changes which might be necessary in this area. The state will play a key role in the regulation of the labour market.

• To articulate an integrated system of material and moral incentives for workers in the socially owned sector. This is a necessary part of any plan to

---

[72]   See Dilla (1993).

raise productivity and intensity of labour. The material component is necessary but not sufficient: monetary reward linked to productivity, with some wage flexibility, is essential. But there also needs to be an ethical component which should have an ideological content and should also be linked directly to the management of the enterprise. In this sense it is very important that the workforce, both collectively and individually, should have a clear sense of the utility of their own work, awareness of the objectives in the short and medium term, of the trust and responsibility which they carry, of team spirit and of the possibility of making their views known within their firm. Also it is necessary to have a system of positive and negative incentives in both material and moral terms.

• To participate more actively and substantially in regional institutions, especially in the local organs of *Poder Popular*, in the planning of economic and social development.

• To maintain and improve the systems of free and accessible medical treatment for all the population.

• To distribute and redistribute income in order to achieve relative economic equity within the population, avoiding large inequalities in the concentration of income and wealth; to guarantee social security for all citizens.

Coherence and Integrity of the Restructuring Programme

The dynamic between the short, medium and long terms and the dialectic between internal and external factors. The financial disequilibria represent only one of the problems which have to be solved, and the rationalisation of internal finances is a necessary but not sufficient condition for the reestablishment of growth and the development of the Cuban economy. The existing financial imbalances are not the cause but the manifestation of economic phenomena which are impossible to correct just with monetary and financial instruments. If these phenomena are not addressed, the basic conditions that can lead to the reproduction of similar problems remain unchanged.

However, no programme for economic recovery can be successful if it is based on a situation of instability. So it is necessary to introduce measures which will restore certain equilibria in the short term, and at the same time introduce a series of structural modifications for the longer term. The restoration of financial equilibria in the short run implies, by its very nature, a set of economic and social costs. But these should be exceptional and brief, and should not be representative of the long-run programme.

Just as the causes of the current situation are not exclusively external, important though external causes may be, so it is also clear that the basic solutions cannot depend entirely on the dynamic of the external sector. The external sector plays an important role in the reproduction of the Cuban economy but it is not the only determining factor either in qualitative or quantitative terms. Given a specific level of influence and functioning of the external sector, economic growth and development can follow different dynamics and trajectories according to other variables which are determined internally to the economy.

Sequentiality and simultaneity. Two aspects of great importance in the restructuring programme are those relating to sequentiality of stages and phases, and to the simultaneity of the actions required at any given movement. Both aspects give the necessary coherence and avoid delays and improvisations.

> *Sequentiality.* The actions of economic policy require a given order and sequence. The measures adopted at each phase and stage need to follow a strategic long-term vision. There are some measures which cannot be introduced until others are in place; equally, the achievement of some proposals necessitates the immediate application of other measures. The sequencing gives dynamic coherence to the whole programme.

> *Simultaneity.* While sequencing is basic to the progress from one phase or stage to another, so simultaneity is essential to measures undertaken within a given stage. This does not necessarily mean that all measures have to be taken at the same time, but that there are certain measures which, because of their degree of interrelation, will only work if they are adopted together. Simultaneity gives the programme its short-term static coherence.

The problem of proportions. It is necessary to maintain a relative balance at the macroeconomic level between the principal sectors of the economy, which, in the case of an underdeveloped and open economy such as Cuba's, may be identified schematically as: the export sector (indirect supplier of means of production and consumer goods *via* international trade); the domestic output of producer and consumer goods to meet basic needs; and the domestic production of incentive goods.[73]

Accumulation (extended reproduction) depends on the potential surplus (basically net exports), in as much as the reproduction of the labour force depends fundamentally on the domestic production of consumer goods and imports. On the other hand, the restoration of high levels of labour intensity and, to a certain extent, the increase in productivity depend on the production and importation of incentive goods.

---

[73] The definition of incentive consumer goods is a theoretical exercise which is only valid for the study of accumulation in a country with the characteristics of Cuba. In practice, this sector cannot be identified in a precise manner and its definition will vary according to circumstances. It is important to understand that at each moment it is necessary to produce goods which motivate labour, beyond those which just go to satisfy basic needs.

The potential surplus – part of which is made up of net exports – is a key determinant of accumulation, but it is not possible unless simple reproduction is first guaranteed. This depends to a large extent on other sectors of social production and on inter-sectoral exchanges.

Since 1990 the level of productivity and the intensity of labour have been considerably reduced, but the relatively high and inflexible costs of reproduction of the labour force have been maintained.[74] This has aggravated the crisis and deepened the financial imbalances, and the restoration of these two factors is necessary for economic recovery. In the short run, immediate economic measures can restore adequate levels of labour intensity, which are the basis for increasing productivity.[75] However, the achievement of higher labour productivity requires modification in the crisis conditions, and is a medium- and long-term process.

For both objectives (increase in intensity of labour in the short term, and increase in productivity in the long term), it is necessary to increase both the supply of goods to meet basic needs and also incentive goods. Incentive goods are not a luxury, nor are they limited to those who aspire to better standards of living. They constitute above all an essential and indispensable part in reproduction, because of the central role they play in developing the intensity and productivity of labour.[76]

The on-going necessity to maintain and increase levels of consumption – for economic as well as for political and social reasons – creates an inevitable tension between consumption and accumulation. In the short run there is no alternative to directing an important part of social product to consumption in order to guarantee adequate levels of labour intensity and the incentives required to increase productivity.

Productive accumulation is necessary during this initial period so that the economic surplus can be increased in the short term – that is, making possible an increase in net exports. The problem is not so much the development of new exports, although this might be so in specific cases, but to implement investments and other economic measures which will permit the growth of the net balance of the export sector. A key criterion in accumulation in order to rise out of the crisis must be the net level of exports through which accumulation takes place. This necessitates a rigorous evaluation of costs of production in the export

---

[74]   This includes the costs of food, housing, clothing, shoes, transport, education, health and other social and cultural activities and social security and other payments.

[75]   Productivity is defined as production per unit of time or per worker, at an average level of work intensity.

[76]   The need to make available incentive goods to encourage higher levels of intensity and productivity of labour is stronger in a socialist economy since, unlike under capitalism, there are no built in negative incentives; individuals, simply because they are citizens, are guaranteed access to health care, education and social security.

sector, which may require a modification in its structure and its participation in the national income.

On the other hand, from the perspective of shares of national product, import substitution must be directed essentially at the modification of the import component of national production (because of the beneficial effect which this will have on the potential surplus) and not to obtain narrow objectives such as the 'liberation' of foreign exchange to be utilised in other priority activities. Any attempt to reduce consumption below certain levels in order to 'free' foreign exchange will have a negative global effect (on intensity and productivity of labour) which will affect the general possibilities of economic reproduction and increase political tensions.

It is therefore necessary to combine an export strategy with a guaranteed level of basic consumption (essentially in the agrarian sector), domestic production of incentive goods (mainly in light industry, metal mechanical, housing construction, national tourism as well as other products and services), and imports aimed at meeting basic needs and incentives. The increase in exports is necessary, but not sufficient in itself, to reactivate the economy.

Since the basic criterion of an export strategy must be the net foreign exchange earnings, in the short term priority must be given to those sectors which are able rapidly to generate greater flows of foreign exchange (traditional exports, and some key sectors) and to carry out investments and adopt policies to promote inter-sectoral development to maximise the net income from other export sectors (particularly tourism). In the long term, export strategy must be oriented towards the creation of new highly dynamic export sectors with high net foreign exchange earning capacity, which may well require key investment in given areas in the short term.

The production of incentive goods and services must become an immediate priority since without these it will be difficult to restore levels of work intensity and achieve increases in productivity. Given the constraints on the availability of foreign exchange, the composition of the range of goods must be resolved in favour of either domestic production or imports – whichever costs less in terms of foreign exchange (this determination is very complex and requires the analysis of relative exchange rates).

Sales of foreign exchange to the population, although increasingly they correspond to incentive mechanisms through employment, are negative to the extent that they distort the role of earnings for the majority of workers (who do not share in such incentive mechanisms), and they should be eliminated. As we explain below, domestically available foreign exchange can be controlled without maintaining a dual exchange system. We do not propose that the holding of foreign exchange should again be made illegal, but that the liberating power of the Cuban peso in the country should be strengthened as much as possible in individual commercial transactions in order to initiate a progressive and rapid movement towards the establishment of a single national currency. The elimination of monetary duality must be a priority element insofar as it represents the degree of freedom necessary to carry out economic policy, given the role the national currency must play in cushioning the economy from the direct effect of international prices.

As we will see in the next chapter, the final objective will be to eliminate monetary duality altogether. Strictly, we would have preferred to achieve this at an early stage of the restructuring programme, but given the concrete conditions of the Cuban economy it will be necessary to maintain the authorisation of certain currency transactions between foreign and Cuban enterprises.

Decentralisation: the dialectic between planning and the market

An underdeveloped economy with a limited supply of resources requires the centralisation of most important key economic decisions implied in planned development. However, the decentralisation of another group of less important decisions is also necessary in order to allow for flexible responses by different economic actors and by the population in general.[77]

As has been demonstrated historically, it is impossible to expand the sphere of autonomous decision-making of firms without at the same time recognising the importance of the market on which to a large extent the premises and criteria for such decisions are based.[78] The planning-market problem is not amenable to extremes or definitive conclusions. An extreme central planning system destroys the flexibility and capacity of operation of the economy. An extreme market system obscures long-term vision and, inevitably, promotes inequalities.[79]

The maintenance and improvement of the planning system is the *sine qua non* of economic development and the reproduction of the political system. But the construction of a market, regulated by the state *via* economic and administrative instruments, is necessary to increase the decentralisation and efficiency of these

---

[77] By *centralisation* we assume a specific functioning of the economic system in which the 'central level' would play a key role within a given hierarchy of economic agents, particularly state agents. In the context of a centralised economic system we take the term 'decentralisation' as a concept which is subordinated to 'centralisation'. So, although 'centralisation' essentially describes the nature of the mechanism of economic coordination of a given type (centralised), 'decentralisation' identifies the degree of relative flexibility which exists in this type of system for different (non-central) state economic agents. The degree of centralisation expresses the structuring of coordination mechanisms in the economic system, although it is also linked to forms of property ownership and intra-firm organisation and control. The high level of concentration of production does not necessarily imply centralised economic systems.

[78] See Brus (1972), p. 83.

[79] This fact has been recognised by the most advanced Marxist and non-Marxist theorists from Karl Marx to Max Weber. Weber observed that 'When the market abandons itself completely to its own legitimacy, it pays attention to nothing but goods, and not to people, and recognises no obligation of brotherhood or pity' (Weber, 1972).

decisions and to connect the diverse economic subjects which do – and must – coexist.

It is certain that according to some theoretical perspectives other alternatives might exist – apart from the market – to decentralise a socialist economic system. In fact, in this context market and decentralisation must not be understood as synonymous terms. The articulation of a socialist economic model can also be stimulated by the conceptions of so-called decentralised socialist planning,[80] which, in spite of general misconceptions, do not just deal with the search for a more participatory socialist model but seek above all the incorporation of a decentralised method of planning. This aspect is central to the understanding of the differences between our own model and other alternative decentralisation projects.

The importance of popular participation as a component of socialist planning has been, at least in theory, a shared component in many different arguments in defence of planning, even though this principle has been devalued in practice. In order to respond to this there has been, for some time now, an attempt to seek a more participatory socialist planning model. However, participation has been only one aspect in the design of alternative models. The character of the coordination mechanism (centralised or decentralised) has been the other important aspect in the discussion. Therefore, decentralisation and greater participation are also not synonymous. In fact the most common of alternative socialist models[81] are models of 'centralised socialist democratic planning', in which the participation of workers and consumers is combined with a centralised coordination mechanism. In general, the role of the market is very limited in such models, and firms operate with few financial restrictions.[82]

The model of 'decentralised socialist planning' is also presented as a participatory model, but planning in this model is carried out without a centralised coordination system. The decentralisation mechanism takes place through inter-firm relations, and the participation of consumers' and workers' councils which operate on the basis of a series of consultations on planning goals.[83]

Popular participation and decentralisation in the economic process have also been the focus of analysis and models by Cuban social scientists, who have addressed these issues from a broad perspective, based on a new socialist model

---

[80]   Albert and Hahnel (1981); (1983); (1990a); (1990b); (1990c).

[81]   These models are proposed as alternatives to the so-called 'bureaucratic decentralised planning' model on which are based most of the socialist economic reforms including *perestroika*. This model introduced two 'decentralising' measures: firstly the reduction of the number of planning indicators, and secondly the reduction in the number of links in the planning chain.

[82]   Some recent proposals on this kind can be found in Mandel (1986) and (1988); and Nove (1987).

[83]   See Albert and Hahnel, cited in footnote 80.

which integrates all spheres of social life.[84] Although the emphasis in most of these studies has been on what has been called the problem of 'decentralisation-socialisation of power',[85] there are also various references to the question of decentralisation in the relatively more limited context of the economic system.

In our view the problem of decentralisation of the economic system necessitates more precise conceptualisation in the Cuban debate, since while there seems to be agreement on certain general aspects relevant to the pertinence of a more decentralised and more participatory economic system, at the same time there is a lack of precision as to the actual decentralisation model that is being proposed. This deficiency is located principally in two areas: the precise nature of economic coordination and the role of the market in the coordination mechanisms.

In regard to the first point, in Cuba the question is not so much whether the actual economic system should be decentralised – since there appears to be ever wider agreement on this point – but *which* model of decentralisation should be adopted, since it is not the same to implant a model of *centralised planning* (which may include a relatively significant aspect of decentralisation) as to adopt a system of *decentralised planning*. Each of these models represents in conceptual and practical terms different responses to a central question about the economic system – its mechanism of coordination.

In addition, the role, expansion and deepening of the market also require greater precision in the debate since the difference between the acceptance of the market limited to its role as a mechanism for the transmission of information and a conceptualisation of the market as a mechanism of direct allocation of resources will be crucial to the shape of the economic coordination mechanism. Our model assumes that popular participation is a socio-political fundamental. It shares a central aim with the models elaborated by other Cuban and foreign authors who have approached the questions of decentralisation and participation. Our proposal shares certain aspects contained in those models – for example, the high level of control of workers over management, popular control of planning and the economic development of firms, and a greater role for consumers.

Our model attempts to introduce a higher level of specificity on the mechanism of economic coordination proposed for the planning process. Our model conceives of a *centralised planning system* with a high level of state linkages, but with a relatively high level of decentralisation centred on a regulated market of the means of production and foreign exchange. In this model the market will be an active decentralising component in the economic coordination of the system. We think that in the current situation in Cuba this is

---

[84] Some of the more significant recent work on this theme are: Dilla (1992) and (1993); Suárez Salazar (1993); Martínez (1993); Alonso (1993); González (1992); Valdés Paz (1993, 1995a, 1995b); Arenas (1994); Martín (1993); and Limia (1992).

[85] See Dilla (1993).

the most appropriate (if not ideal) system to re-articulate an economic system responding to the actual necessities of the economy and to popular aspirations.

A tacit recognition of the need for economic decentralisation in the current situation is demonstrated by the growth in own-account work and the creation of the UBPCs, and the establishment of the farmers' markets and the industrial and artisanal markets.

In the recent experience of Cuba, the most advanced experiment in inter-enterprise organisation has been that carried out by the military enterprises of the Armed Forces, known as 'business improvement schemes' (see Annex 3). This has succeeded in putting in place a more efficient system of business administration, based fundamentally on decentralisation. However, this experience has shown the need to establish a market so that the decisions taken by the firm can take effect.

Under these conditions the acceptance of a larger presence of the market would seem to be necessary for the Cuban economy, accentuated by the actual and future conditions in which it has to develop:

a) the growing presence of foreign investment, and the relations with foreign economic subjects operating under market principles;

(b) the expansion of non-state forms of production such as own-account workers and cooperatives;

(c) the need to seek higher productive efficiency within state enterprises *via* decentralisation, and to achieve a more efficient distribution of resources in the global economy.[86]

The gradualism of the construction of this market is a premise of the articulation of a socialist model of the economy with a higher degree of decentralisation. The formation of the market in a more abrupt form – the so-called 'big bang' – will increase the economic, social and political costs and make this alternative non-viable, even in the context of the dominance of state ownership.

In the economic sphere the sudden development of the market without a realistic starting point, in the absence of developed institutions, and without taking into account possible imperfections of competition, or trained management capacity, could lead to a high level of enterprise failure and an 'adverse selection' in which the most efficient enterprises would not necessarily be the winners. This would affect the claimed greater allocative efficiency which the

---

[86]   There is an extensive literature which argues that it is necessary to utilise market mechanisms in a planned economy. See, among others, W. Brus (1972 and 1985).

market ought to guarantee. Even worse, the various problems that the state would have to deal with following the sudden development of the market would prevent the state focusing on the sectors that might generate greater dynamism in the economy. In sum, in the context of a 'big bang', the interventionary capacity of the state, which is necessary to compensate for the deficiencies of an immature market, would be reduced. From a political perspective this would generate levels of unemployment and inflation that would destroy any public support for the project.

We are therefore talking about a process of growth of the market, in which it will play a major role in the distribution of productive resources but without substituting for the fundamental role of the state planning system in overseeing the whole economic system. This is only possible with a radical modification of the traditional mechanisms of economic planning which, in addition to what has been discussed above, will require a greater role for regional planning – an indispensable element in the state's actions in the context of a system of economic coordination with higher levels of decentralisation and participation.

The planning responsibilities of the state comprise three main areas:

Strategic planning. This is the prefiguration of the development of the country in the long term, taking into account different possible scenarios. It has to identify the principal variables on which it is necessary to act in order to direct the process along the path to achieve the national project.

Directive planning. This has two dimensions:

> *In centralised areas:* this is exercised in relation to centralised state firms (see below) and budgeted units,[87] and involves investment in physical and social infrastructure as well as direct productive investment in maximum priority areas. Planning targets for key indicators are present.

> *In decentralised areas:* this is exercised on decentralised state firms, cooperatives and private firms. It is carried out through state contracts which firms are obliged to fulfil. In principle, these would refer to minimum production targets or services generated by different state enterprises.

Indirect planning. This has two dimensions:

> *Macroeconomic:* this is exercised at the national level by means of the regulation of external economic policy (exchange rate, tariffs, subsidies

---

[87] These are state units which produce goods and services whose principal objective is not the generation of incomes or profits. In general these include schools, hospitals, research centres etc.

etc.), monetary and fiscal policies, and control of prices and wages, to achieve macroeconomic stability.

Microeconomic: this is exercised on economic entities by means of monetary and fiscal policy, prices policy, labour norms, commercial and environmental policy, applied in differentiated form in given branches, firms and territories.

Business Reform

Ownership and forms of organisation of production. In the economic sphere the construction of socialism in Cuba meant a double process. On the one hand, there was a series of fundamental changes in the social relations of production, and on the other the enactment of changes in the forces of production to ensure the levels of material production necessary to satisfy social needs.

In the experience of the Cuban Revolution the problem of the articulation of different forms of ownership (state, cooperative and private) was very early on resolved in favour of state forms of ownership and organisation.[88] This sector has been totally dominant and decisive in the reproduction of the economy and the social achievements of the country over the last three decades; at the same time it also explains some of the problems existing today.

The process of cooperativisation and privatisation in given spaces in the economy – which has already started in Cuba with the creation of the UBPCs and the expansion of own account-work and foreign investment – will continue to develop through the following instruments:

a) the sale of state assets to cooperative and private agents;
b) the removal of entry barriers for non-state agents in areas of the economy previously reserved for the state;
c) the contracting of non-state agents for part of the productive process: contracts for administration or services previously carried out by the state, renting of assets and contracts of concessions which do not necessarily involve sale of state assets.[89]

However, the current economic situation and the change in the international

---

[88] In spite of the difficulty of precise definitions, in this book we understand by 'private' sector the range of economic activities undertaken by individuals or families as own-account work, individual peasant farmers and small and medium-sized enterprises, and foreign companies. We define the 'cooperative' sector to include owners or tenants who operate as direct producers and participate in the collective management of the entity, and share the profits; this includes those enterprises which employ wage labour, as long as the cooperativists are the direct producers.

[89] For a discussion of these instruments, see Gutiérrez (1994).

context emphasies the problem of the articulation of different form of ownership. The growing coexistence of state and non-state forms of ownership appears to be an inevitable process in the actual situation.

When diversification in ownership occurs by means of a ceding of rights without a transfer of ownership – such as in the case of land authorised for utilisation by the UBPCs recently in Cuba – new forms of production are created and their regulation acquires a new significance. The cooperative form of these new units differs from the previous state form, but at the same time it is a path which limits the possibility of capitalist development in agriculture since it converts cooperative members into their own labour force and leads to the possibilities of accumulation and use of acquired rights. Similar formulae could apply to other productive sectors or to service providers.

In the current conditions of the country, the search for better levels of economic efficiency raises the necessity for the establishment of new forms of ownership. However, the socialising essence of the Cuban project requires the preservation of the dominance of social ownership. Its predominance needs to be a central element of the model to guarantee the socio-economic development of the country according to national interests, and to sustain the necessary social expenditure which will permit decent standards of living for the mass of the population. Within this context forms of private property should be articulated in the non-fundamental means of production, as a structural rather than a conjunctural element, when they can guarantee higher levels of efficiency and employment within the limits established for their control.

It is necessary to take into account that a central economic problem in the re-articulation of different forms of ownership is the mode of appropriation of economic surplus. To be more precise, with a given level of 'retreat' or 'concession' in the realm of property ownership – of means of production, or of output, or both – it is crucial for the socialist state to 'advance' in terms of the mechanisms which will determine the modes of appropriation of part of the surplus in non-state forms of production.

In terms of future development, the growth in productivity – in particular for individual producers – gives rise to the possibility of many new advanced forms of production for which the state needs to establish policies which could facilitate this process. It also needs to establish mechanisms to provide social security for those working in non-state sectors.[90]

In our proposal the dominance of social ownership (state and cooperative sector), which currently coexists with the small and medium-sized firm, is secured by keeping state ownership as the fundamental ownership form in the

---

[90] For example, at present no such mechanisms exist for people in so-called own-account employment.

large sector which is made up of the most important of the country's enterprises. However, as we see below, state ownership will acquire new characteristics which will differ from those adopted throughout most of the history of socialism. Now there will be a greater level of decentralisation and a greater participation of the workforce in both the management and the profits of the enterprise. The *Juntas de Administración,* which we discuss below, will be a basic part of the articulation of the interests of the enterprise and the wider interests of society.

Scales of production

The technology available is in the last instance what will determine the degree of concentration of production in order efficiently to utilise economies of scale. There are three levels of concentration of production:

a) *Natural monopoly.* A single enterprise which can produce all or nearly all of the required output of a good or service, which is the most efficient form of organisation. Such firms require a high level of capital.

b) *Oligopoly.* A single firm is insufficient to produce the total level of production, because unit costs begin to rise before social demand is satisfied. In this situation the optimal outcome would be the coexistence of a limited group of firms in the same activity. This will also generally require a high level of capital.

c) *Multi-firms.* A high level of concentration of administration and production is inefficient. Unit costs begin to rise at small scales of production. It is necessary to maintain a large number of firms. In general they require low levels of capital.

The possibility of establishing *a priori* the optimal scale of production and making this coincide with the optimal degree of concentration of administration is an advantage of state management of the economy.

The problems of the optimal scale of production occur at different levels. Within domestic markets with no foreign competition it might be good to encourage competition between firms, but where there is competition from foreign trade the state could merge previously independent firms and encourage competition with foreign firms. This requires the state to have discretion to intervene.

Strategic advantages are concentrated in the monopoly and oligopoly sectors and those which could manage an advantageous entry into the international market. The firms which function in these sectors can develop as state enterprises given the social importance of their production and their capacity to generate economic surplus and the high level of capital required, though in some cases they may allow the use of certain non-state forms of organisation that do not imply transfer of property ownership. Partnerships with foreign capital should be permitted when lack of resources, technology and markets make this necessary, a process in which it is necessary to establish institutional procedures which can guarantee consultation with *Poder Popular* at its different levels.[91] From the political point of view the dominance of social ownership has a basic importance in the reproduction of the sociopolitical system.[92]

In a sector in which there could coexist many enterprises, different forms of ownership are possible – state, cooperative, private,[93] individual and mixed. This includes services to the population, minor production and the greater part of agricultural production. This structure recognises the importance of the small and medium-size cooperative enterprise under forms of mercantile production.

In the conditions of a socialist project it is necessary to impose limitations on private enterprise, to prevent it growing excessively. The limits to its expansion need to be set by the amount of capital and the number of employees, differentiated by economic sectors.[94] If a given firm reaches its determined limits, and it is in the social interest that it should continue to grow, it should be required to seek an association with the state.

The question of how to reconcile the establishment of limits on small and medium-size firms with their active role in the functioning of a socialist economy is one of the challenges of restructuring. At a given moment, the accumulation of capital of these firms should be restricted to the limits under which they have been established, both by their own expansion and by the growth associated with the state, which could lead to undesirable consequences such as the loss of interest in production, the failure to realise their productive potential, the search for illegal alternatives or the temptation to export capital.

---

[91] Also the central government could propose, after the widest consultation, the establishment of a series of norms which would facilitate the transfer of ownership to foreign capital in order to solve the most urgent problems of the balance of payments. This would not necessarily be linked to the conditions for access by foreign capital delineated above.

[92] This will guarantee social ownership – juridical and economic – of the basic means of production. This would eliminate the possibility of the predominance of a new bourgeoisie and would ensure national independence in the face of the interests of foreign capital and governments.

[93] In the context of this book we understand by 'private ownership' any form of organisation of production in which private control is held over the means of production, and labour is contracted. This is differentiated from individual ownership in which the labour process is carried out by the individuals who own the means of production, or with the help of family members, without contracting labour. Although until now the Cuban government has no clear definition of whether private national enterprises are acceptable, the possibility has been admitted by state officials, for example in the speech of the Minister of Economy and Planning during the second conference on 'La nación y emigración' held in Havana at the beginning of November 1995. See *Trabajadores*, Havana, 6 Nov. 1995.

[94] Here we make only a general reference to the different criteria which could be used to establish limits on private enterprise. The quantification and regulation of these limits will depend on detailed analysis which is beyond the scope of this book.

In our view the creation of possibilities of investment in the financial sphere could be seen as a way to resolve this problem. This would allow the continuation of the accumulation of capital, but in an area separate from the concrete sphere of activities of private firms (the accumulation of capital), and at the same time would channel this to areas which are compatible with the principles of a socialist economy – in particular the establishment of mechanisms for issuing bonds of different types (enterprise, development, municipal and others)[95] and consequently for the creation of a bond market. Given that bonds do not confer ownership rights, this would prevent greater expansion of direct private control over physical assets. This would be preferable to share issues.

The functioning of small and medium-size private enterprises should not be seen as any form of retreat, but as a pragmatic utilisation of the most appropriate form of ownership in the concrete conditions in which the country has to develop. Such a move would also resolve a paradoxical situation from the political point of view – the right of Cubans who have left the country to invest has been recognised, while serious restrictions remain on investment by residents of Cuba, among others the ban on contracting labour.[96]

Different types of firms

According to the criteria listed above three types of firms can be identified:

Type A Firms

These will be firms whose scale and technology are monopolistic or oligopolistic. They are very important because of the impact of their particular branch or activity on the rest of the economy. They generate large amounts of economic surplus or are concentrated in activities which are strategic to the country's development. Those firms which are defined as Type A are state-owned and are directly controlled by central government, i.e. they are centralised firms. Only exceptionally is foreign capital permitted.

Their centralised administration does not imply that these firms might not achieve a degree of autonomy, but important decisions do need to be taken, or approved, by the central government. Their principal characteristics are:

a) They are directly controlled by the ministries.

---

[95]   The issuing of bonds would not just be a desirable channel for private investment, but would also permit private sources to be used to finance investment programmes of wide social benefit.

[96]   By capital investment we understand activities aimed at producing surplus value. This is a complex theme which is highly sensitive in political and ideological terms and we have not expanded on it in this book. We have restricted ourselves to indicate that we consider this to be a conceptual problem which must be taken into account in order to resolve a contradiction of current economic policy.

b) Central government plans their fundamental activities. They will be required to comply with the following indicators, among others:

- production targets in determined supplies and proportions
- prices of goods and basic services
- salaries of the principal executives
- investment
- indicators of profitability.

Central government will decide on their mergers or dissolution and will appoint the chief management. However, within these limits they will have more autonomy than at present. Degrees of flexibility must exist within the planning indicators.

c) In general they must attend to two fundamental objectives which, on occasion, will appear to be contradictory:

- to meet certain social objectives, which could affect their profitability either permanently or in the short run
- to achieve a reasonable level of financial profitability.

The simultaneous pursuit of both objectives requires close attention by central government. Because of the social importance of their activities, it is the government rather than the market that must force them to comply with these objectives.

Type B Firms

These are firms which are oligopolistic by virtue of scale and technology. However, unlike Type A firms their impact on economic relations in the country is not of the first order, or they are in activities which do not require direct supervision by central government, having reached a high degree of competitiveness. Although Type B firms may be state-owned or joint ventures (with participation of foreign capital) they are essentially defined by the fact that they are not under the control of Ministries, but under 'Administrative Boards' – *Juntas de Administración* (see below) – whose members are nominated by the organisations of *Poder Popular* at different levels according to the geographical location and importance of the enterprise.

In this type of enterprise, as well as for state firms of Type C, state ownership will be exercised *via* the participation of the workforce in the management of the enterprise in a more direct form than hitherto. They should be profitable and respond in large measure to market signals.

Since they are oligopolies, these firms can be the source of distortions in the market for well known reasons: oligopoly prices and lower production levels than are socially required. But in this case they will also be subject to certain regulation by central or local government (provincial and municipal) or both, concerning price ceilings for some products, and the obligation to meet certain stock levels, quality norms and work and wages regulation, environmental protection etc.

In spite of the direct influence of the government at different levels, this will be less than for Type A firms. The different government levels (central, provincial and municipal) will send signals to these firms *via* the market by means of economic instruments such as credit or taxation policy. The ministerial control of these firms would be negative in operational terms since it would inevitably imply direct interference.[97]

In summary their principal characteristics are:

a) They are directly controlled by Administrative Boards (*Juntas de Administración*), set up by national, provincial or municipal assemblies of *Poder Popular*, with responsibility for financial control and the development of a long-term strategy for these firms, which can be state-owned or joint ventures.

b) Central and – under the direct authorisation of the former – local government will retain the capacity for direct regulation of these firms, but will exercise it *via* economic mechanisms, e.g. discretionary shares, price ceilings and stock control of given products. These firms will retain a high level of autonomy and a part of their profits to reinvest through their own decision.

c) Mergers/takeovers will have to be authorised by central government in order to avoid degrees of concentration inimical to the functioning of a market in the context of a socialist economy.

d) The principal objective of these firms is to produce profitably and to function with the highest level of efficiency, operating in competition with other firms.

Type C Firms

These will be small and medium-size firms, which by virtue of their characteristics of high levels of concentration of ownership and administration are inefficient or uncompetitive. Their average costs would begin to rise at quite low levels of production. A large number of such firms can coexist even if they

---

[97]   Alonso (1992) observes 'Real or historical socialism, when it turns the state into the owner and administrator, stifles the control of ministers and other state organisms and produces a race by civil servants to become businessmen'.

produce the same kind of products or services. They generally require little capital. These types of firms are characterised by their decentralisation and can operate under various types of ownership – state, cooperative, private, individual or mixed.[98]

The principal characteristics of Type C firms are:

a) In the case of state enterprises, they will be controlled by Administrative Boards, nominated by assemblies of *Poder Popular*. Given their reduced scale the appropriate level is the municipality. In the case of non-state-owned enterprises, the owners can decide the form of organisation.

b) They will operate basically according to market signals, although local or national governments retain the prerogative to impose price ceilings, under central government authority. The government's role in regard to such firms will be to create conditions for them to operate efficiently *via* markets.

c) Their principal objectives are to function profitably and efficiently.

In the case of privately owned firms their growth will be subject to the limits noted above (capital, number of employees, obligatory association with the state after reaching a certain size).

Type B and C state-owned enterprises will be under the control of local *Poder Popular* units; profits will go to the local organisations of *Poder Popular*, in addition to transfers to the central budget, reinvestment for development, and profits shares to management and workers. This will ensure that local management will maintain vigilance over these firms and will play an important role in the decentralisation of state management. In the case of bankruptcy such firms can be dissolved according to legal regulations that will be established for such cases.

Administrative Boards ('Juntas de Administración')

Poder Popular, at its different levels, represents the interests of the whole population and must therefore play a central and active role in the management of state-owned firms. However, like their counterparts in the national, provincial and municipal assemblies, representative bodies of *Poder Popular* cannot concentrate their time on the management of these firms, nor do they necessarily possess the relevant skills. They will therefore set up 'Juntas de Administración'

---

[98] In this type of firm, generally the owner and the manager are the same. The case for the necessity to develop small and medium-size firms is beyond the limits of this book and has been addressed by the authors in greater detail elsewhere.

comprised of directors and workers from the firm as well as external members, all of whom will be selected by the appropriate Assembly of *Poder Popular*, at national, provincial or municipal level according to the sphere of operation.[99]

The external board members could be 'outstanding workers' (*obreros destacados*), national or local personalities, scientists, finance and banking professionals or other relevant specialists. Customers and users of services, and also the local community, should be represented in the *Junta de Administración*.[100] These boards will not interfere with the daily operation of the enterprises but will periodically evaluate their development from a long-run point of view.[101] They will validate the decisions of the management and act as trustees for state property, and they will receive additional payment for this function. Members of the Boards do not have to be professionals, but will be selected for their high civic vocation and their skills and will keep *Poder Popular* up to date with developments in the enterprise.

Foreign investment and enterprise organisation

At present and for the foreseeable future, foreign investment constitutes a variable which cannot be excluded or minimised in any consideration of the national economy. According to the degree of participation of foreign capital in the formation of enterprises, these may be joint ventures or, exceptionally, wholly-owned foreign enterprises.

In September 1995 a new law of foreign investment was approved with the objective of consolidating the process of foreign investment in the country, informed by the practical experience of recent years.[102] The dynamic of this process requires regular revisions of the legal framework which, as well as bringing up to date the legislation currently in force, would permit the establishment of a more transparent and precise juridical context in conjunction with other regulations.

Central government will propose to the National Assembly of *Poder Popular* a National Programme for Foreign Investment which should be periodically

---

[99] For a more detailed examination, see the chapter 'Los consejos de Administración', in Haimann and Scott (1997). The inclusion of worker representatives in the boards, elected by the workers themselves, gives them an important role in the running of the firm. There is an extensive literature about the passive role of such boards in the management of firms. Without ignoring this, we think that the functioning of the Administrative Boards in our proposal is a step that must be taken. For a view on complementary measures to ensure the better functioning of management boards, see Roemer (1995), pp. 107-9.

[100] One of the advantages of having external members is that these could evaluate the enterprise objectively without being directly involved in its operation. Another advantage is that they can coopt high-level specialists who work in other firms and organisations.

[101] cf. Haimann and Scott (1977).

[102] In the first edition of this book, we made the case for a new law of foreign investment.

revised. This programme will define, among other things, the sectors in which foreign capital should be permitted and the relation between foreign investment and the rest of the national economy. In this way the National Assembly of *Poder Popular* will have the ultimate control on policy for foreign investment. Any firm with foreign investment of whatever type must in general comply with the same regulations as national firms:

- If they carry out activities in monopoly or oligopoly sectors over which central government exercises direct control (Type A companies), they will also have to fulfil extensive requirements concerning output targets, price ceilings and tariffs. Decisions concerning expansion will remain in the hands of the state.

- If they are active in other sectors they will be subject to the same regulations as other economic agents.

In all cases they require government approval and government decisions will define tax policy and other conditions according to established regulations. An important factor for consideration in policy concerning foreign investment is its effect on the productive links within the domestic economy. This question is implicit in the previous discussion on net exports; however, there is a particular dimension to this problem which requires special attention: the role of an industrial policy,[103] especially designed to promote and optimise the development of such productive linkages.

There are two types of linkages – forward and backward. In the case of foreign investment, the former is linked to productive networks which confer value added to products and services arising in the first stage from foreign investment, whilst the latter refers to the generation of economic activities aimed at meeting the input requirements of foreign capital, for example supplying the tourist sector. In practice, both types of linkages are produced simultaneously and, if they are promoted effectively through specific policies, can lead to the creation of an economic 'shelter' in which foreign investment can be inserted, with the additional benefit that its presence contributes to the functioning and stability of the national economy.

An adequate utilisation of the potential which foreign investment offers to activate such links assumes the application of a raft of measures, which range from the elimination of the dual nature of the economy to the establishment of various policies in areas such as exchange rates, tariffs, procedure for legalising contracts, technical standards and regulation for consumer protection, among others. However, more important than the management of instruments available

---

[103] By 'industrial policy' we understand actions of the state designed to promote or discourage specific sectors, branches or enterprises in any area of the economy, not just in industry. Note that the term 'industrial' here means more than the usual statistical definition of the industrial sector of the economy.

to administer industrial policy with the aims stated above is the comprehension that foreign investment is not a sector isolated from the rest of the economy, nor one whose only function is to make good specific gaps in capital, technology and markets.

The contribution of foreign capital can be positive or negative and the final balance will depend on the degree and manner in which it is inserted into the national economy. In an 'open' and underdeveloped economy such as Cuba where, moreover, foreign investment is concentrated almost exclusively in the export sector, the tendency for a negative 'contribution' to national income can be reinforced.[104] At present this phenomenon is influenced by the absence of effective measures to link foreign investment with a broad group of Cuban firms which could potentially act as suppliers of goods and services required by foreign capital. However, the principal problem is the persistence of dual structures in the economy, limiting the possible connection between foreign investment and the rest of the economy, and adding to the low utilisation of direct demand and the wasting of the potential induced effects that could be derived from these investments.

The resolution of the dual structure of the economy is a necessary condition for the maximisation of the benefits of foreign investment and industrial policy must be directed towards encouraging such links with the national economy.

Mechanisms of Regulation and Redistribution

Company finance

Historically, in the model of a centrally planned economy, including that applied in Cuba from the mid-1970s, the compliance with production plans was more important than the search for productive efficiency or quality improvement. According to conceptual analysis of this phenomenon, in particular the well-known works of the Hungarian economist Janos Kornai,[105] the reason lies in the existence of soft budget constraints within the model.[106] Therefore, it is

---

[104] Another important aspect is the effect of foreign investment on the balance of payments. However, we have placed the emphasis here on the relationship between foreign investment and the national enterprise system.

[105] For a short but clear exposition of Kornai's position, see González (1993).

[106] In Cuba's case, a clear manifestation of this has been the high levels of matured loans accumulated by state enterprises, which have their origins in exaggerated levels of money in circulation (stocks and accounts owing), and in real losses or losses above planned levels. In fact the problem is even more serious if we take into account that other activities not included in 'operational accounts' of the enterprises, such as investment payments, have also generated high levels of fixed assets (idle or under-utilised) which are not reflected in their current financial balance; but even without these the result is still seriously negative. However, in theory and in practice the state enterprises could be as profitable as private firms in an economic context which forces them to be efficient and which guarantees them autonomy. Studies carried out abroad are not conclusive in

necessary to construct a system of hard budget constraints which will encourage the search for profitability and excellence in quality control.

The four central components of such a financial system should be:

– The existence of real negative and positive incentives on the basis of company autonomy. The negative incentives will be given by the possibility of bankruptcy, regulated by a Law of Bankruptcy and the removal of personnel with inadequate financial skills from company management. The 'positive' incentives would be increase in profits, the possibility of expansion of such firms and the salary levels for management and workforce.[107]

– The companies' Administrative Boards and the bodies which control *Poder Popular* will play an active role in financial regulation. Part of the profits of decentralised firms can increase budgets at different levels. On the other hand, central government must ensure that centralised firms are also subject to control according to social and financial objectives.

– The creation of the Bank of Commerce and Development, which will operate according to enterprise principles, will play a very important role in the selective authorisation of credits and in ensuring their repayment. The elimination of indiscriminate subsidies which the state has frequently granted will make credit an important source of finance, linked to the generation of efficiency under these new conditions.[108] The development of a state capital market will also reinforce the necessity to seek new levels of profitability in order to expand the company.

– Competition will be a primary factor in the achievement of efficiency and will enable the survival and expansion of companies as a function of their profitability and the improvement in the quality of production. There is sufficient evidence at the international level that competition plays a more important role than ownership in achieving productive and distributive efficiency.[109] Competition is not just domestic, but as the economy is gradually opened external agents will become involved in competition, increasing the pressure to achieve efficiency within enterprises.

---

regard to the role of ownership in the improvement of efficiency, an issue which is deliberately ignored by those arguing for privatisation. See Jones (1991) and Salazar (1991). See also Vernon (1989); Gutiérrez (1995).

[107] The idea that only the private sector is able to create 'positive' or 'negative' incentives for efficient management is one of the assumptions of neo-liberalism and can be found in many of the proposals for Cuba's development which have been produced outside the country. For a documentation of this notion, see Bartell (1993) and Martin (1988).

[108] This does not imply that subsidies cannot be given to certain enterprises. The state can also act to support certain firms to avoid bankruptcies, but under rigorous conditions of financial probity.

[109] See Martin (1993); Devlin (1993); and Adam, Cavendish and Mistry (1992).

Macroeconomic equilibria

The existence of strong financial controls at the microeconomic level is a necessary precondition for macroeconomic equilibrium;[110] on the other hand, macroeconomic stability is a necessary condition for stability at the level of enterprise development and the achievement of global economic goals: growth of output and employment, low rates of inflation and external equilibrium.

Of course, within our restructuring model, which assumes that the market will act as a mechanism for the distribution of resources, the management of macroeconomic equilibrium is more complicated. Administrative decisions about distribution will be replaced in many cases by 'signals' sent by the state to the market to be processed by economic entities in order to guide their activities in the desired direction. In this way coordination of monetary and fiscal policies, external economies, and price and wages policies acquire a central role in the success of restructuring.

In Cuba's case, given the central role of the state sector, the budget surplus assumes a crucial role in macroeconomic stabilisation. Austerity in spending and its adjustment to the real economic situation, tax policies which permit fiscal balance or the existence of manageable imbalances are also central to the success of restructuring.

The role of taxation

The exercise of the fiscal functions of the Cuban state requires a substantial restructuring of the sources of budget income, particularly of taxation. The creation of new permanent sources of income to replace other sources, which have disappeared or which are dwindling, both stabilises a renewed fiscal base and involves designing a new taxation system that will include mechanisms for accounting, recording and control of taxation and of tax avoidance. In a situation where a range of different forms of property ownership coexist, taxation policy acquires a central role in macroeconomic stabilisation and the achievement of social equity.

Public health and education – free and universal – are major shares of budget expenditure in Cuba; because of their universality they impose a 'neutral' burden on a large part of social expenditure in that by nature they are not a compensatory type of expenditure which will lead to income redistribution in favour of certain population groups. In this situation the progressive nature of the net fiscal burden depends on taxation policy. Progressive direct taxation on

---

[110] A too weak system of financial restrictions at the microeconomic level will generate inflationary processes and external disequilibria, such as occurred in the 1980s in Hungary, Poland and China during the process of decentralisation of enterprise management. See González (1993).

personal income and profits of enterprises must have a central role in this.[111]

Within our restructuring policy there are three elements which will determine the evolution of taxation policy:

– the degree of concentration of non-state production, which will have an important effect on the possibility of introducing changes in tax policy while minimising tax evasion;

– the creation and consolidation of a legal, institutional and fiscal framework;

– the growing importance that non-state forms of production will need to have (up to a determined limit);

The distinct elements that will characterise fiscal policy at each stage of the proposed restructuring programme are detailed in Chapter 4. Here we review certain conceptual generalisations:

– Progressive taxation on personal income and wealth will play an important role in the taxation system (this will include wages, benefits, dividends, rents, interest, remittances in foreign exchange and all other forms of personal income and property, including inheritance). Wages should not be discounted as possible sources of tax in that it is foreseeable that a decentralised economy may produce significant differences in wages; but in the present conditions of the country, the other options available should be fully exploited before a tax on wages is imposed.

– The contributions to state income made by state firms represent a dividend payment to the enterprise owners (the state) rather than taxation. However, from the conventional point of view, contributions to the state budget by enterprises of Types B and C will formally acquire the character of taxation. These firms will retain part of their profits for their own development including profit sharing to the workforce. The rest will be divided between the level of government (municipal or provincial) to which the enterprise is subordinated, and to the central government budget.

– In Type A enterprises that have decentralised, the tax system will be similar to Type B and C enterprises.

– Non-state firms will be taxed on profits, and this can also contribute to local and national budgets.

– UBPCs and state agricultural enterprises will pay rent on land, and

---

[111] By 'progressive' is meant a fiscal policy aimed at redistribution of income in favour of lower income groups.

individual farmers and other agrarian cooperatives that are land owners will pay tax on their land values, both payments depending on factors such as the quality and location of the land.

– A tax could be established on the net worth of enterprises (e.g. buildings, equipment) in order to reduce the risks of tax evasion that are present in taxes on personal and company income. In addition, this will encourage more efficient use of resources and contribute to regional planning.

– At a later stage in restructuring, Value Added Tax (VAT) could become a key element in tax income, that is somewhat progressive *via* exemptions on goods of basic consumption. VAT will replace specific purchase taxes (for example, on cars and restaurants). Nevertheless, it is necessary to introduce a note of caution concerning VAT. This must not take over the central role occupied by direct taxation in the tax structure. The collectability of VAT depends on reliable recording; without an effective mechanism of organisation and verification of income, it could easily lead to tax evasion by the business sector.

– Indirect taxation on luxury goods and services will also be a progressive element of taxation policy and encourage savings.[112]

– All enterprises (whether or not state-owned) will contribute to the social security of their employees.

– The focus of benefit[113] could also be used to fix some indirect taxes (e.g. fuel).

– It is advisable for taxes to be concentrated on a limited number rather than a wide range of taxes. This saves on the costs of fiscal control and simplifies the evaluation of the progressive or regressive character of the tax – a particularly complex task when there is a wide range of taxes.

– Local taxation will be an effective instrument for decentralisation of state expenditure; the proportion of taxation which will remain at local level will vary according to regional planning and other circumstances; however, this will not exclude the possibility of transfer from central government.

– The development of a high degree of capacity for control by the state, in particular concerning the verification of income declarations, is a key factor in the adequate functioning of a taxation system which is needed in a more diversified and decentralised economy. This should reduce tax evasion to the minimum and ensure the progressive character of the tax system. In Cuba's

---

[112]   The meaning of 'luxury' will be modified as the restructuring process evolves.

[113]   This is one of the existing criteria used to establish tax levels, in this case paid by those who benefit from a good or public service, for example road transport, bridges and tunnels.

case we must assume the design and implementation of the institutional structure that would guarantee the realisation of these functions. Here we include everything from the development of the recently created National Office for Tax Administration (ONAT) to the reform of the banking system.

The role of the state

In the situation in which there has been a process of decentralisation in the running of state enterprises, and simultaneously there have developed non-state forms of production and services in which the market plays an important part in the distribution of resources at the microeconomic level, the state must readjust its functions at all levels and give greater emphasis to the use of economic instruments. The state will retain its protagonist role, but will exercise it in a much more complex way. Its functions will then be:

Planning. It will coordinate administrative and indirect planning methods. The rest of its functions will be subordinated to these. Central government, with the active participation of local government, will specify long and short-term plans. Centralised enterprises (Type A) are a direct instrument for implementing such plans, while economic mechanisms and state contracts[114] for certain supplies will help other economic agents to achieve their goals. Planning determines the principal shape of the economy.

Promotion. It will promote the development of branches and firms *via* investment, credit policies, protectionist duties, tax policies etc., and the development of specific regions.

Regulation. It will establish the rules of the market: anti-monopoly regulation, contract rules, price ceilings, quality standards, consumer protection, regulation of foreign investment, ownership regulation, environmental protection, minimum wage, arbitration system, etc. State regulation of labour rules and conditions, in particular, is necessary to avoid the negative impact of the market on the workforce.

Investment. It will invest in enterprises directly under its control. However, it may also carry out direct investment in other productive sectors even when there are decentralised, non-state enterprises in these areas. In such cases, if the consequence of such investment is the creation of a new enterprise the state must decide whether or not this remains under direct state control. The state may also invest so as to share with companies the risk of investment in an uncertain scenario.

---

[114] State contracts could be carried out in conditions of preferential prices for enterprises, and could in certain cases involve the award of contracts with participation of state, private and cooperative sectors.

The state will carry out investment in physical and social infrastructure. Tendering processes can be transformed into a mechanism for selecting the implementers of central investments. In any case, whatever the decentralising mechanisms introduced, the state will retain the key roles in investment:

Entrepreneurial. The state will act directly on state-owned centralised and decentralised enterprises and can also become a partner in non-state enterprises. Its role as direct administrator is essential in strategic activities.

Banking. Through the Bank of Commerce and Development, which will be a Type A enterprise, it will have discretionary control over credit policy and the development of specific activities.

Stabilising. The state will act as a stabiliser through control of monetary policy *via* the Central Bank, fiscal policy *via* taxation and expenditure, price and wage control and foreign trade policy *via* import licences, customs duties, exchange rates etc. This will be aimed at achieving high rates of growth of production and employment, avoiding high inflation and maintaining equilibrium in the balance of payments.

Redistribution. The state will carry out policies of income distribution *via* progressive taxation and subsidies to certain sections of the population. It will supply health and education and thus determine the share of national income devoted to social consumption.

A highly skilled central and local government is required to carry out these functions, some of which are entirely new, and also the necessary institutions to control such economic activity. It is important to emphasise that direct investment by central government, even in the decentralised sectors, is of utmost importance.

In summary, the capacity of the state to guarantee the socialist objectives and content of economic restructuring are expressed in the following ways:
   a. retaining the ownership of basic means of production;
   b. planning the objectives, rates of development and structures of the economy;
   c. defining a system of rules to regulate monetary exchange relations;
   d. carrying out a fundamental role in the functioning and implementation of investment;
   e. establishing and controlling an enterprise system for the country;
   f. establishing and controlling employment and wage systems;
   g. guaranteeing the social expenditure necessary to maintain and develop basic social gains;
   h. approving and controlling foreign investment.

These functions will need to be distributed and exercised at different levels of government.

CHAPTER 4

The dynamic of economic restructuring

The programme of restructuring set out in this chapter has been developed on the basis of the concrete conditions of Cuba's economy, society and political situation, and in the framework defined by the principles enunciated in the previous chapter. This programme needs coordinated action in defined areas and a specified timetable, characteristics which distinguish it from other proposals for reform which are not based on an awareness of the socio-political reality of the country, start out from different premises, pursue objectives which differ from a socialist project or have not been thought out as an integrated long-term programme.

The scope and complexity of restructuring which will ensure the continuation of the socialist project in Cuba require different decisions at different stages. In the following pages we outline one of the possible alternatives for the development of restructuring. Progress from one stage to another will depend on a variety of factors which go beyond the economy. The movement of the restructuring process will be determined in large measure by processes derived from the interaction of social subjects who will react in different ways and intensities to the changes. We will not go into this very complex process here; we have limited the analysis of the advance of the programme through its different stages to the consideration of factors more directly linked to the economy.

In this sphere the speed of transition from one stage to another will depend on two fundamental factors:

– The restructuring of state enterprises which must take priority, because of their key position in the economy. Their efficiency must be continually improved not just *vis-à-vis* other forms of ownership and national production but also in relation to foreign investment. This will also depend on the increase in the efficiency of subsidised units which will allow for increases in the levels of quality, production and services within assigned budgets. This will require rigorous control of costs and outputs.

– The evolution of the external sector which will allow for necessary levels of imports for the reestablishment of productive and social infrastructure, the decentralisation of control of state enterprises and the development of a socialist market. The lifting of the economic blockade imposed by the United States, an increase in foreign investment and access to international credit would have considerable impact on this. Given the open character of the Cuban economy, the dynamic of the external sector will be an important variable in the definition of the possible trajectories of economic recovery and therefore in the context in which we have to develop the restructuring programme. The objective of the restructuring is to give the Cuban economy a system of economic relations which will permit it to achieve to its maximum potential and, rather than obstruct, will dynamise the development of forces of production.

We have divided the economic restructuring programme into three stages. The first will be developed in two phases. The first stage is presented in greater detail than the other two which are more long-term:

Stage 1: restitution of financial equilibria and search for efficiency.
  Phase A : rationalisation of internal finances
  Phase B : initiation of economic restructuring

Stage 2: transition to a regulated market

Stage 3: decentralisation of the economy.

Each stage reflects the different emphasis which must be placed at any given moment on economic activities. In this sense the structural changes in the first stage are aimed at stabilisation and economic rationalisation and are distinct from the structural stages of the following stages which have more ambitious objectives.

With the exception of Stage 1 phase A (rationalisation of internal finances), which we estimate will take about one month, we cannot make exact predictions of the duration of the other stages and phases for two reasons: first, because the speed of transition depends on factors previously listed (which are subject themselves to great uncertainty); secondly, because we would need to work out a much more detailed elaboration of various aspects which are only sketched out here.

Of course, determining time periods is a central issue. If it is negative to adopt time frames which are too brief (with the exception of the first phase), which will prevent the consolidation of the results, excessive gradualism is also problematic. In particular, we must take into account that Phase A (rationalisation of internal finances) is unavoidable and must take place as quickly as possible, because the recessionary nature of this part of the programme carries social, political and economic costs which must not be prolonged any longer than is strictly necessary.

In the presentation of each of these stages the corresponding objectives and instruments will be defined. Each stage will focus on specific areas of action except for Phase A of the first stage, which will comprise a broad range of precise measures. Although we have tried to identify precise objectives and policies in each stage, specific aspects will have to be redefined as we proceed.

We must make clear that the restructuring project which we propose here only defines the most general aspects of the measures to be adopted in each stage.

In each stage and phase it is essential to construct a coherent legal framework with the structural changes which must be implemented. This requires a definite institutional effort, in order to clarify the rules of participation and responsibility.

The restructuring of the economy requires an industrial policy which will impact at each stage on sectors and specific enterprises *via* the use of economic instruments (customs duties, import permits, selective credits, direct assignment of foreign exchange, state contracts, state investment in dynamic sectors etc.). It is important to define the sectors in which import substitution will be encouraged in the context of the country's industrialisation and the gradual lifting of regulation on protected activities.

In economic restructuring the state will not be limited to correcting the classic market 'failures' (imperfect competition, presence of externalities and social inequality, amongst others). In all cases the market will be subordinated to planning in order to 'force' the development and guarantee the primacy of the state sector and of political power in the hands of the people.

The project presented below has a logical system, i.e. each of the measures described will not have the same significance and effectiveness on its own as part of a coordinated economic programme. This is not to say, however, that each of the measures has to be adopted in exactly the form suggested in order for the programme to function. There is a degree of flexibility in the articulation of the components of this programme, as in all economic programmes.

The spheres of action[115] will be:

1. reform of state enterprise
2. re-articulation of other forms of ownership
3. social security
4. price and wage policy
5. exchange rate policy
6. budget
7. foreign trade
8. banking: monetary and credit policy
9. state investment

---

[115] Other spheres of action could have been chosen. Strictly, the practical application of this programme will require modifications in areas not covered by this proposal. However, we consider that the spheres of action selected are the most important and those which cannot be ignored in any fundamental economic reform programme for the Cuban economy. Nor is it intended that this proposal will detail the complete process of articulation of the participatory democratic socialist model that must accompany the implantation of the new economic model.

Stage 1: Restitution of Financial Equilibria and Search for Efficiency

This first stage has the following basic objectives:
- amelioration of internal finances
- increase of agrarian production
- achievement of greater efficiency in the enterprise and budget systems.

This stage will have two phases:
Phase A : amelioration of internal finances
Phase B : initiation of economic restructuring

Between phases A and B we have to solve the problem of immediate continuity. Taking into account the brevity of Phase A the measures contained in Phase B must be prepared and quantified in general terms before Phase A commences. Certainly Phase B will take no less than a year, and may take longer. This phase can be planned in detail in the course of development on the basis of the general project defined in this book.

Phase A: Amelioration of internal finances
The issue of improvement of internal finances has been the most discussed to date in all sectors of the country. This phase, crucial for economic restructuring, is composed of a package of measures which are either simultaneous or follow each other very closely.

The general measure which will be used during this phase is the initial contraction of demand and its subsequent maintenance at a level compatible with the real levels of supply to the population, together with a reduction in the fiscal deficit (*via* retail prices).[116] The programme for this phase should be implemented in a relatively short time period (about a month) and should create conditions to minimise inflation in the following stages.

a) *Currency substitution*

Currency substitution is a central measure to achieve the demonetisation of the economy necessary to ensure the viability of the whole process of adjustment.[117] Demonetisation at the beginning of the restructuring project will

---

[116] Since supply of consumer goods from state firms is dominant, the increase in prices automatically constitutes an increase in income for the Treasury.

[117] From 1 June 1994 the Cuban government implemented a series of measures designed to reduce excess money in circulation, the most important of which are: the increase in the price of various goods and services (tobacco, alcohol, electricity and transport); charges for services which previously had been free (school meals, entrance to museums, utilisation of sporting facilities, water and sewage services, some types of education etc.) In the view of the authors this type of gradual 'demonetisation' will lead to an even greater polarisation of cash, and to a concentration of the reduction in demand among employees in the state sector and a tendency towards the depression of recently legalised non-state sectors. One of the basic premises of the version adopted by the authors

confine the recessive effects of this measure to the initial phase and reduce the complications which its later application could inflict on the process of restructuring aimed at producing a sustained recovery in economic activity.

In particular the implementation of monetary exchange in the initial phase favours the creation of conditions which will improve the effectiveness of the state sector and is an indispensable premise for the construction of a market which is not based on a perverse distribution of cash. At the beginning of the restructuring project the state sector, which is dominant in national output, is still not functioning under financial pressures since the allocation of resources is carried out in a centralised manner and current liquidity only plays a secondary role. On the other hand, one of the basic starting points of the restructuring is an unequal distribution of money, which in large measure benefits those people who have violated the law; this situation needs to be changed since if not it will produce a reconcentration of income which will put this section at an advantage in filling the new spaces being created in the market.

This phase of demonetisation will permit the combination of the advantages of avoiding an abrupt paralysis of the activities of state firms (which will not be greatly affected by the modification in the level of available money supply) with the creation of a framework which will, nevertheless, have a beneficial effect on the functioning of companies in later stages when measures will be adopted to bestow a real and effective role on such firms. Moreover, the measures to reduce money in circulation will be more successful at the beginning than at later stages of the restructuring programme when the state sector will have a larger role and will be seriously affected by the abrupt reduction in demand.

The proposal that we put forward here forces the burden of adjustment to be

---

is that demonetisation must take place *before* any other measure to promote the creation of markets, particularly if they are associated with non-state competition. This was the idea proposed in our previously mentioned work, in April 1994. The introduction of a gradual demonetisation scheme as adopted in Cuba encourages the creation of markets before achieving a sufficient level of demonetisation of the economy. In this context the version that we have chosen here, equivalent to a replacement of currency with confiscation, will be more complicated to implement because of its negative effect on the dynamic of sectors such as agriculture. This is a clear example of the importance of sequencing of measures. The recognition that the implementation of the plan selected here presents practical difficulties in the current context does not mean, however, that the authors consider that this is not the most appropriate option. The most important thing is that the rest of the programme retains its validity in the concrete conditions prevailing in Cuba, even if the form of demonetarisation actually applied in the country does not coincide with what we have proposed. In spite of this we have to take into account that even in the present conditions the version proposed can be applied, but in a modified manner – for example, with the exemption from confiscation of bank balances after 1 October 1994, the date of the introduction of the farmers' markets. Even in this case measures of forced saving should be applied to these surpluses. In Chapter 5, below, we analyse in more detail the demonetisation plan and the various alternatives available in reality. We also set out the basis for the option we have chosen, of currency exchange with partial confiscation and at progressive rates of exchange.

carried by those sectors of the population holding the greatest share of the money supply (see Annex 4, which analyses how the majority of legal accumulations of money are the result of market distortions). This is crucial from the political point of view, since it will not impact on the majority of working people.[118]

There are different alternative models for monetary exchange.[119] Having analysed the economic effectiveness and political costs, we recommend the following:

– exchange of all existing cash, both in saving deposits and in the hands of the population;

– cash could be exchanged for the new money in regressive proportions, staggered on the basis of given quantities (see Table 2);

Table 2

Example: process of exchange for an individual who has 4,000 pesos in cash and 27,000 pesos in bank deposit accounts		
Cash in hand	**Proportion of exchange**	**Post-exchange cash**
First 2,000	1 x 1.00	2,000
From 2,000 to 20,000	1 x 0.33	5,940
More than 20,000	1 x 0.10	1,100
Total		9,040

Note: The intervals and proportions of exchange utilised in this example are only to facilitate comprehension and do not represent a prescription for monetary exchange.

– all cash exchanged above a given level must be deposited in a bank account and only a certain amount would be authorised to be withdrawn in a given time period;

---

[118] It is evident that a confiscation policy is threatened by leakages. Those who have concentrations of money will try to disperse it to avoid the exchange controls that may be established. To deal with this, secrecy and speed in these measures are important.

[119] Among the options available is to exchange the whole sum of money presented, but to require an obligatory deposit of any amount that exceeds a given level. This money could then be withdrawn later in partial amounts over a certain periods. This option would achieve an initial demonetisation, although it represents a *de facto* 'economic amnesty' for those citizens who have accumulated cash by illegal means or thanks to distortions in non-state markets. In periods following the restructuring, the political cost of this option could be high because those sectors of the population that benefit particularly are those involved in renting or sale of shares in Type C enterprises, and/or in the development of the market which will permit the growth of consumption or private investment.

– to validate the exchange of money above a given limit, its holder must be able to demonstrate the legitimacy of its sources; if he is unable to do so, everything above the established limit will be confiscated;

– in the case of citizens such as peasant farmers or other sectors for whom cash is also productive capital, different proportions of exchange and a special system of withdrawal of deposits can be established, provided that they are used for productive investments or other purposes in accordance with the priorities of the economic policy;

– bank deposits will not be indexed;[120]

– deposit accounts in foreign exchange will be permitted.[121]

b) *Reform of consumer prices*

This measure will include:

– maintenance of a policy of rationing for basic products, the list of which should be systematically revised as a function of the level of supply;

– increase in prices of rationed basic products, by eliminating or reducing subsidies. Even if these prices should not be fixed by supply and demand (after demonetisation), they should be higher than current price levels;[122]

– immediate change to a system of free sale of available products which are not basic necessities, such as services of cafeterias and restaurants, tourism, petrol for private use, alcoholic beverages, tobacco.[123] These should have prices fixed by the state, taking into account the relation between supply and demand. This measure will be as much directed to the construction of a parallel market[124] as to the closing of certain over-profitable areas of the

---

[120]   The non-indexation of these deposits represents an additional instrument of demonetisation since future price increases will lower their real value.

[121]   In 1995 the Cuban government authorised the opening of foreign exchange accounts by Cuban citizens.

[122]   The fundamental objective will be the reduction of budget deficits, but the determination of the prices of these products has political and social implications which require consideration of their possible impact and the evaluation of different systems of subsidies, the relative weight of subsidies in the total price, and their compensation *via* other fiscal incomes.

[123]   Some of these products were transferred to free sales as part of the financial rationalisation measures introduced by the Cuban government in 1994.

[124]   The term 'parallel market' is commonly used in Cuba. Within it the prices of consumer goods offered by the state are fixed according to supply and demand. The term 'parallel' signifies that it coexists with the rationing of some of the goods which are offered at subsidised prices. After the beginning of the so-called 'Special Period', this market was eliminated and practically all consumer goods were distributed *via* rationing. The articulation of a parallel market minimises or eliminates the necessity of payment in kind or in convertible currency 'certificates' that some authorised

informal market.[125]

The above does not exclude the possibility that some proportion of these goods and service can be made available through rationing at differentiated prices (e.g. petrol for private cars, cigars).

These measures will reduce the gap, even if they do not totally close it, between state supply and effective demand. They could also have the result that they affect the section of the population with lowest incomes. To overcome this the state will have to apply measures of protection and compensation which we will examine later.

c) *Maximum reinforcement of the unlimited use of Cuban currency for transactions within non-state national sectors*

The holding of foreign exchange will be legalised, but with an attempt to maximise the utilisation of national currency in national non-state sectors. This will reduce the circulation of foreign currency and other modes of liquidity (including foreign exchange certificates[126]) in these activities.[127] This measure would be more radical than the variation proposed by other specialists for the establishment of a convertible peso at par with the dollar, an intermediate step that we believe should be avoided.

As we have already noted, the ideal would be to eliminate totally and from the start the circulation of foreign currency but the complexity and diversity of the current economic reality makes it impossible to achieve this by means of administrative measures, particularly in the sphere of transactions between consumers and non-state sectors.[128] Neither would it seem sensible to eliminate totally, from the start of the programme, foreign exchange transactions that state

---

enterprises currently give their workers.

[125]   This reordering of prices will allow the reduction in the share of cash captured in duties on items such as tobacco and alcoholic drinks to be compensated by a higher level of profit on other products sold by the state. Taxation on alcohol or tobacco has a clearly regressive character.

[126]   For many years foreign exchange certificates of various sorts, issued by the Cuban government, have circulated in Cuba, permitting access to scarce goods and services offered in a limited network of establishments. The dollar started to circulate gradually and, following the de-penalisation of dollar holdings in mid-1993, its use was extended. In 1994 December the convertible peso was created and replaced the circulation of different types of foreign exchange certificates, and its use as a medium of exchange is 'as good as' the US dollar.

[127]   Other specialists consider an intermediate step necessary in which the convertible peso will circulate as a substitute for the dollar without initially breaking the monetary dualism which exists. The creation of the convertible peso in January 1995 was directed towards this alternative. Although we think that this was a step forward, we think it is possible to proceed directly to the circulation of a single national currency.

[128]   Although in practice part of the relations between consumers and non-state sectors is conducted in foreign exchange, technically the Cuban state has to compensate any consumer who complains that he has been denied access to goods and services in national currency, and from the legal point of view the Cuban currency has unrestricted exchange value for the payment of all liabilities incurred within the national territory.

entities carry out between themselves and overseas entities. In the current conditions of the country, and the requirements of company operations, a radical change of this sort could exceed the possibilities of rapid assimilation of the new context on the part of the entities involved. However, the elimination of the circulation of foreign exchange in sales between the state and individuals will contribute in a decisive manner to the reinforcement of the utilisation of foreign currency. In spite of the note of caution introduced above, it should be clear that the complete elimination of monetary dualism should proceed as fast as possible. This action will give the population access to goods and services (many of which are imported) which at present are only available in exchange for dollars or foreign exchange certificates.

Under this proposal people who receive remittances and other incomes in foreign exchange, together with foreign residents and tourists, will have to change money for national currency to make payments. This will be made possible by the application of a special exchange rate for such purposes.[129] (To understand the conditions which will facilitate the establishment of this exchange rate, see Annex 5).

This is the first measure necessary to eliminate monetary dualism. However, payments in foreign exchange between certain enterprises in the state sector and between these and foreign firms investing or involved in Cuba's overseas trade will be maintained.

The national currency will not be convertible in this first phase, except by authorised foreign firms and some national enterprises (e.g. the tourist sector) for given purposes (e.g. repatriation of profits, certain imports, and functioning of foreign exchange self-financing schemes). This is a central measure in motivating labour and making links between tourism and other state and non-state sectors to promote growth in production and employment. With the implementation of this and other measures included in part (b) of this phase, a parallel market in goods and services for the population will be reactivated.

d) *Programme of minimum income for individuals and social sectors affected*

In principle subsidies should be applied to individual or family units, rather than to products. They should be directed to the satisfaction of minimum necessities of food, clothing, housing etc. of all individuals whose family income *per capita* is below a previously determined level, and to certain social sectors requiring special attention: pregnant women, old people, people with physical and mental disabilities etc. The conditions should be created for the gradual establishment of social security mechanisms for non-state sectors. In particular, a programme

---

[129] The application of a special exchange rate, different from the official rate used in other transactions, will also mean the use of a specific rate in state enterprises and joint ventures with foreign capital in the tourist sector in order to convert foreign exchange into national currency. This will require the establishment of certain regulations and controls.

of social security should be established immediately for own-account workers, financed by contributions from this sector.

Phase B: Initiation of economic restructuring

As we have indicated, the restoration of the necessary financial equilibria must be followed by more profound structural changes which will consolidate them and reactivate the productive apparatus of the country through the establishment of conditions designed to generate a new growth dynamic.

Reform of state enterprises

In the initial phases of restructuring it is of the utmost importance to make centralised control of state enterprises as efficient as possible in order to create a socialist market in later stages.[130]Actions in this area will be as follows:

a) Generalisation of the principles of enterprise management tried out in military enterprises, known as 'business improvement' ('perfeccionamiento empresarial'), suitably adapted for the rest of the state system. In no way is the general introduction of this system contradicted by the subsequent development of the enterprise system, which will tend towards decentralisation. Its extension should increase productive efficiency.

The military system has given great importance to developing a system of incentives designed to secure fulfilment of targets, with flexibility in their determination while retaining some financial profitability of the firms. The greatest innovation of this system of enterprise management is the reward or penalising of management, in relation to financial profitability among other criteria.[131]

The rewards of the workers will be in direct relation to the results of their work. Thus, the variable part of their wages will play an important part in their motivation. Formulae linking variables such as reduction in costs or increase in quality to the individual earnings of the worker must be developed. Also moral incentives for good results and discipline must play a central role and labour indiscipline and non-fulfilment must be penalised in some fashion.

One of the principal sources of increases in efficiency in the recent

---

[130]   In the former Soviet Union, during *perestroika* the government ceased to exercise effective control over state enterprises and at the end of the 1980s there was neither planning nor a market but total economic anarchy.

[131]   In various military enterprises using a system of 'improvement', a system of incentives has been tried in which administrative personnel share a percentage of the profits if they fulfil targets. The workers, at the same time, share part of the profit obtained through reduction in unit production costs.

experience of military enterprises has been the reduction of their staff levels. Some of the excess work force have been redeployed in other useful tasks. This process, if carried out at the level of the whole economy, will leave a considerable number of workers without immediate redeployment within the state sector of the economy. These people, as we will see further on, can find opportunities within the non-state sector or obtain social support. In no case will they be abandoned.

b) Study of enterprise activity to allow the classification of enterprises according to Type (A, B or C) and the planning of their future control similar to the process for other types of non-state property. One of the objects of this study will be the determination of the optimal scale of enterprise to avoid unnecessary monopolies or oligopolies and the current autarchy at ministerial level.[132]

c) Analysis of enterprises which are currently unprofitable and the possible concentration of production in a smaller number of entities. This is one of the most complex tasks since many of these loss-making enterprises function with prices which make them artificially non-profitable given current distortions, whilst others carry an excess labour force or suffer from extreme disorganisation of production. This could be overcome or improved through a process of rationalisation. In any case, given that price reform necessary to eliminate distortions will take time, in the first instance evaluation of effectiveness can be carried out in terms of foreign exchange[133] or the comparison of costs between enterprises in order to decide whether a given firm should be shut down.

d) Cooperativisation or privatisation of enterprises of Type C wishing to undertake this. Measures such as sales by auction, renting and administration or service contracts could be considered. This should be carried out gradually, following the analysis described in b) above. There may be certain key economic activities, such as agriculture, industry and commerce and others including services which are amenable to a cooperative solution. Other activities of less

---

[132] Today there are a number of large firms and conglomerates of firms created 'artificially', not in accordance with optimal degrees of concentration of production, but to facilitate centralised control by ministries. The latter delegate functions of distribution and control of resources to these units. Also a common feature in Cuba today is for ministries and unions to possess automobile workshops or construction or catering units etc. This brings with it a certain autarchy in provision of services. In the experience of the military enterprises undergoing 'improvement', this arrangement was stopped and specialised enterprises were created which supplied producer services to permit more intensive utilisation of the means of production.

[133] Because of the clear distortion of domestic wholesale prices and the existence of an exchange rate which has not had any economic basis, for many years there has been a system in Cuba of evaluating productive efficiency in foreign exchange terms. This consists in comparing production with its costs, both valued directly in international prices. The big disadvantage of this system is that the cost of labour and other costs related to national value added reflect very imprecisely foreign exchange costs. Nevertheless, this method could be useful in the initial stages of the restructuring programme to evaluate activities in which the cost of imported direct inputs (especially raw materials) exceeds the value of the level of national production, when both are compared at international prices.

economic importance, such as cafeterias, shoe mending, barbershops and hairdressers, carpenters, automobile workshops, small firms etc. – that is, sectors that provide services and minor products to the population – can adopt cooperative or private forms.

Enterprises of Type A or B could contract services from cooperatives or private firms for the provision of certain activities such as administration, dining rooms, maintenance, installation of software etc.

e) In this phase, when the state and non-state sectors still function under different logics, the link between these sectors should be encouraged, but under strict regulations to avoid corruption or the obtaining of price subsidies by non-state agents.

Re-articulation of other forms of ownership

a) Extension of UBPCs' decision-making and improvement in their autonomy. This measure is important for the increase in agrarian production. It will be necessary to advance the autonomy of these units by means of the following:

– Fixing of volumes and prices of sales to the state and authorisation of the sale of excess production to the market at equilibrium prices. This market can also supply state agricultural firms, cooperatives and private peasant farmers.[134]

– The terms of the relationship between the state and the UBPCs must be fixed legally and interference in the autonomous decision of units that contradict agreements must be avoided.[135]

As part of the general reform, the prices of UBPC stock must be continually revised to keep them in line with the prices at which the state purchases their products and with inputs in order to minimise distortions in the benefits of the non-state sector. The state will have the discretion to fix price ceilings in the markets for certain agrarian products.

---

[134] The creation of the farmers' markets in October 1994 coincided with this part of our proposals.

[135] Decree Law 142 of 1993 established an important structural change in Cuban agricultural by the transformation of state farms into UBPCs *via* the grant of the use of state lands to labour collectives. However, limits were imposed on the managerial autonomy of the UBPCs which had to supply 100% of their production to the state at fixed prices. In practice, in addition to these restrictions, the state firms and other enterprises continue to interfere in the decisions of these units. The establishment of the farmers' markets in October 1994 followed the same lines as earlier proposals of the authors of this book. These markets represent a step in the right direction towards overcoming the difficulties of the first year of the UBPCs, but the complexity of their problems requires additional methods, particularly the redefinition of their relations with the state, the supply and quality of their labour force and their access to certain consumer goods.

The three first measures adopted in phase A (monetary exchange, price increases and limitation on the circulation of foreign exchange) will act as a catalyst to re-incentivate agrarian production.

b) Flexibility of own-account work and acceptance of other forms of ownership. As we noted above the transference of ownership of Type C enterprises, as well as administration or service contracts in Type A or B firms, should be a route for the re-articulation of the non-state sector. Given the conditions of demonetisation in the economy, for the time being the sales of state assets could be carried out in stages or using frozen bank deposits. There will also be space to form small private enterprises and cooperatives in authorised sectors.

Having achieved the first phase, the super-profits which the informal sector can currently obtain will, in the process of formalisation, be considerably reduced. The taxation system will help in this. The decentralisation of the economy,[136] as well as encouraging initiative, will allow a progressive growth in production: from self-employment to small and medium-size private or cooperative firms. Beyond this level, there will be limits that have been described in other parts of this book.

The barriers to entry which Resolution No. 1 of the CETSS-CEF imposes with respect to who can carry out own-account work and the prohibition of employment of wage labour should be modified. The reduction in the barriers to entry in this sector will allow the incorporation of a greater number of people with the following three positive effects:[137]

- absorption of surplus labour from the state sector
- increase in supply of goods and services
- price reductions as a consequence of increase in supply.

The development of cooperatives and small firms requires an intermediary to link the producer and the consumer. The reemergence of this agent could help the development of small-scale production.[138]

However, there is a problem in this process whose solution is very limited in the first stage: the creation of a market in materials and means of production for small-scale non-state production. The initial sources for this market in the first stage will be:

---

[136] As we noted above, in October 1994 the Council of Ministers issued Decree No. 192 authorising the creation of markets for industrial and artisanal products from 1 December 1994. This measure is compatible with the restructuring proposal set out here and will facilitate its adoption.

[137] In mid-1995 new legal regulations were issued which authorised the extension of own-account enterprise, including Resolution No. 10/95 of the Ministry of Labour and Social Security, dated 30 June 1995. This permits university graduates to work in own-account enterprises, though not in their own profession, which in our view still represents an important barrier to entry.

[138] With the creation of the farmers' markets the figure of the intermediary – now called the representative – has begun to reappear.

- the market for agricultural goods
- the parallel market for retail sales
- direct sale by the state of materials and resources which previously were assigned to state sector enterprises of Type C, but which are now under various kinds of non-state organisation
- direct sale by the state of excess resources.

In every case the sale of materials and equipment by the state should be at free market prices (and in some cases by auction). This element is important to avoid the transference of hidden subsidies to the non-state sector. On the other hand, it requires a reinforcement of the control of state enterprises and stores to avoid theft and diversion.

Skilled labour should also have the opportunity to form companies or cooperatives of professionals, such as accountants and consultants, which can offer services to the nascent non-state small businesses and, at later stages, also to state firms. In this phase of the programme a bankruptcy law should be enacted covering private firms and cooperatives.

Social security

It is likely that there will be a large number of unemployed at the beginning of the enterprise reform programme, in spite of the development of small private or cooperative firms. For this reason, as well as the programme of minimum wages detailed in the first phase – which will guarantee access to minimum basic needs to all affected individuals and sectors – the state will have to take additional measures to deal with the surplus workforce:

- re-training for their future incorporation in other sectors
- subsidies which will guarantee part of the previous wage levels, under the conditions that the person will carry out useful work in the community for a fixed period, until they are redeployed
- reorientation to labour-intensive activities.

Additional methods which will contribute to an increase in employment could include the temporary installation of *maquiladora* firms in Cuba and the export of high-skill services.

The adoption of new social security measures would be appropriate, designed specifically for own-account workers and private and cooperative companies (in the case of private companies this would be on the basis of employee contributions). Individual retirement plans for the owners of these enterprises would also be established.

Price and Wage Policies

The measures taken in this phase would be:

a) The realisation of a general price reform in the state sector to eliminate current distortions. The process that has been started in Cuba through the introduction of variation in international prices in the definition of domestic prices is totally compatible with the programme proposed here.

The determination of national prices should be preceded by rationalisation of enterprises and should take into account actual rather than ideal conditions of production. Thus, they should include an adjustment according to the different sectoral levels of profitability and lead to a narrowing of the gap between wholesale and retail prices.

This reform should be carried out as an integrated process, to include the determining of an economically justified exchange rate. This will result in the modification of domestic prices and an exchange rate that will allow appropriate assessment of real national production compared to goods produced outside. The new prices should be an instrument for correct microeconomic decision-making in relation to the closure or promotion of certain production facilities, according to the industrial policy adopted.

The permanent incorporation of changes in import prices will lead *per se* to the introduction of international inflation. This logically would generate the necessity of mechanisms of indexation for wages and social payments. The improvement of the price system should be a permanent task, intimately linked with economic recovery.

b) Maintaining the line adopted in the first phase in relation to prices of consumer goods.

c) Establishing in a discretionary manner price ceilings for some products in the farmers' markets and for other products where the degree of concentration in the commercialisation of the product allows this.

d) The initial demonetisation of the economy will create necessary conditions for a reform of wages in the state sector that should be directed at achieving a greater differentiation between the minimum and maximum wage levels.[139] This will eliminate payments in kind which have proliferated in recent years. There also needs to be a permanent reform to reconcile supply and demand of labour in productive and unproductive sectors, and to stimulate the more skilled workers. The achievement of this equilibrium is an important premise for proceeding to the second stage. In addition, 'participative' wage schemes[140] should be encouraged according to the economic results of the enterprises

---

[139] In Cuba, for example, the nominal salary for a cleaner is 100 pesos a month and for a Minister 450.

[140] In order to increase productivity in the state sector the utilisation of participative wage schemes should be encouraged that depend on the result of individual work effort and the profitability of the enterprise; this will assist the flexibility of management of the state sector.

measured by profits, rates of return and meeting planned production quotas.

Exchange policy

The principle of incorporating modifications of international prices of imports into the determination of domestic prices will ensure the existence of exogenous inflation. However, the predominance of the state sector, which at this stage will still not be functioning under market principles, and the management of fiscal and monetary policy, must avoid endogenous inflation. This will then create the premises for the adoption of an economically justified single exchange rate for all transactions within the national economy. This rate could either be neutral or have a bias towards exports, and could be revised periodically.[141]

The adoption of this single exchange rate for all transactions will make viable in national currency the relations between the national sectors (private, cooperative and state) with foreign capital. However, since the policy of generating high levels of national savings on the basis of 'austerity consumption' will lead to a relative increase in prices of consumption goods, it is necessary to maintain a differentiated rate for tourists in order to maintain international competitiveness in this sector. Monetary dualism must be maintained in this phase, keeping the schemes of foreign exchange self-financing and the administrative redistribution of foreign currency to state enterprises and institutions not included in such schemes. The national currency should not be convertible, except for the enterprises listed in the first phase.[142]

Budget

In this second phase, it will be necessary to achieve a budgetary equilibrium or manageable levels of deficit. In addition to the elements aimed at reduction of the deficit outlined in Phase A, the following will be added:

a) An austerity policy for budgetary expenditure without affecting the fundamental services for the population. This will require a detailed analysis of activities, which in many cases are overmanned.

b) Beginning of the restructuring of the state apparatus in accordance with its changing functions (reform of state enterprise will have important implications) and reduction of its staff levels.

---

[141] The devaluation of the peso can therefore be foreseen. However, economic recovery – if export-led or fuelled by capital inflows – could possibly increase the relative value of the national currency.

[142] An additional problem to resolve is whether to link the national currency with a single foreign currency or with a basket of currencies. The variant selected will depend on the structure of foreign trade by country, the stability of these currencies and the objectives of domestic policy. This requires a more detailed technical analysis which is outside the scope of this work. See Davis (1992).

c) Reduction of subsidies to state enterprises and increases in contributions of profits to the budget as a result of the price reforms, increases in efficiency and closure of unprofitable enterprises.

d) Tax reform. The proposals for tax reform set out in this book were conceived before Law No. 73 of the Taxation System was issued in September 1994 which is very similar, with some small differences, to that proposed here. However, it is important to point out that in the specific context of our proposals, the application of tax reform has important connections with other components of the programme that we think it is important to make explicit.

In state enterprises still not operating on market principles, the retention of part of their profits and the establishment of a profit tax will not have a real economic effect on their functioning during this stage. Investments will be centralised in this phase and the decentralisation of funds will have a formal character, although bank credit could play an important role in the financing of investments.

In a general manner during this first stage the total profits from these state enterprises will influence the budget. However, the firms under a self-financing scheme could incorporate, on an experimental basis, a tax on profits parallel to those for firms operating under other systems.

Private peasant farmers and cooperatives that own land should pay tax on land values and, in the case of the UBPCs and state agrarian firms, there should also be a tax on profits. The land tax should take into account factors such as the quality and location of the land.

Self-employed workers, small private firms, cooperatives and peasant farmers will pay fixed duties during this stage in the form of licences and access to certain points of sale. These charges will have a discretionary character and can be modified according to circumstances. Employers' responsibility for the payment of contributions to social security must be introduced in all sectors of the economy (state and non-state).[143]

---

[143]   This is one of the most important differences between our proposal and Law 73 of the Taxation System. In this first stage the progressive taxation on personal income and property will be relatively light and the state firms will be flexible in their administration. Having established responsibility for contributions to social security on behalf of employees predominantly in the state sector, this will have to support a much wider social service burden. The total burden of contributions by employers will be transferred to consumers through cost of production and services, which will make these payments more equitable in the first stage. Moreover, the imposition of personal taxes on state employees in conditions in which they have been adversely affected by the current situation, is likely to be greatly opposed. It should be recognised that, although the possibility of such a measure has been discussed, up to the present time it has not been introduced. At later stages, payment of a part of this by employees should be assessed in terms of the economy, the growth of real wages in the state sector and the progressive or regressive character of this contribution. The basis on which contributions are calculated – this could be added value, rather than

In this first stage the creation of organisational, institutional and fiscal conditions to carry out a thorough reform of the taxation system will be necessary and this process has already started in Cuba with the adoption of Taxation Law No. 73.

In a situation of a weak direct tax system, indirect taxation applied to luxury items, and in particular on foreign exchange earnings,[144] will give tax policy a progressive tendency.

The imposition of fixed-rate taxes on the non-state sector must take place within determined limits that should be established empirically, not just theoretically: a lower limit that promotes equity and an upper limit that does not discourage production or investment.

Foreign Trade

Given the importance of foreign trade for Cuba and the special difficulties of modifying this in recent years, the restructuring programme must dynamise and develop from the start a series of actions to favour the restructuring programme already being undertaken in the context of the 'economic opening' applied by the Cuban government.[145]

These actions must remain in place at all stages of the programme and for this reason we only note them here, assuming them to be permanent; we will detail only those measures which are of particular salience for the present stage. Among the most important of these permanent actions would be:

– Institutional improvement of the demonopolisation policy in foreign trade and the strengthening of an active enterprise scheme. The concession of trading rights to productive enterprises in Cuba as a result of the decentralisation of the organisation of trade will create institutional conditions to facilitate negotiations between Cuban and foreign enterprises. Such decentralisation does not represent a simple formal change, since the concession of trading rights to productive enterprise leads to a reduction in scale and a more integral focus and greater flexibility in decision-making.

– Continued development of mechanisms to provide solutions, in different ways, to the *impasse* of Cuba's external debt. In particular Cuba should, where possible and appropriate, make use of debt swaps.

---

size of salary – should also be analysed in the taxation imposed on employers. For a discussion of this, see CEPAL (1992), pp. 213-34.

[144] The establishment of taxes on foreign exchange incomes, in particular monetary remittances from abroad, should only be adopted after a study of the effect of such a measure on the flow of remittances. A tax came into force in January 1996 on foreign exchange income that excluded, among other things, remittances.

[145] See Monreal and Rúa (1993).

– Promotion of international agreements, especially Agreements of Partial Access, of economic complementarity and any other agreement which will offer Cuba relative security in access to markets, terms of trade and finance of trade.

– Application of innovatory schemes of business dealings with the creative employment of business formulae ranging from the financing of trade operations and the utilisation of barter trade, to the agreement of economic links between Cuban and foreign firms.

– Development of an adequate commercial infrastructure to promote trade links in competitive conditions. The carrying out of this objective ranges, necessarily, from the creation and continuous extension of regular lines of air and marine transport, the improvement in the technical conditions of ports, airports and warehousing to the provision of competitive port services. Other important elements are the development of telecommunications, and the development of firms of consultants which offer legal and technical services, such as pre-feasibility and feasibility studies as a support for business decisions.

– Continuation of the development of up to date information support on opportunities and reciprocal possibilities in the field of trade and investment, particularly the creation of business data bases and links to international commercial information networks.

– Continuation of the development of 'aggressive' promotion campaigns to promote direct links between Cuban and foreign businessmen.

In addition to those listed above, there are other actions that are relevant in this first stage, as follows:

– Maintenance of the scheme of self-financing and subsequent allocation to enterprises that do not directly generate foreign exchange. This implies the retention of the quasi-monopoly position of the state in foreign trade during the first stage in sensitive areas such as the allocation of foreign exchange. One must remember that, on the one hand, entities that operate self-financing schemes are state enterprises subject to rigorous exchange controls and, on the other, the government maintains a central role in the direct allocation of this resource which is so scarce in the rest of the economy.

– On the basis of price reform and the calculation of an exchange rate which is economically sustainable, customs duties should be revised according to the industrial policy adopted. This should result in modifications in duties – increases as well as reductions. This means putting duties on what is presently exempt. Although at this stage customs duties will play a relatively passive role in the state sector, this provision is important as it is a premise for the gradual opening to foreign trade which will occur in later stages.

– Customs duties could be used as an instrument to ensure the efficiency of national sectors and as a mechanism of international negotiation.[146]

– Price reform will in itself permit important changes in the structure of imports in so far as it is possible to evaluate the relative efficiency of national production in terms of industrial policy.

– The elaboration of sanitary, agricultural, plant hygiene and environmental norms according to the necessity of continuing to implement an ordered trade opening.

Banking: a monetary and credit policy

Separation of the Central Bank and the Bank of Commerce and Development.[147]

The Central Bank should have the following functions:
- control of foreign exchange reserves
- money supply
- exchange policy
- receipt of credit from official sources
- establishment of policies such as preferential credits from different sectors, types of differentiated interest rates etc.
- supervision of the operations of the Bank of Commerce and Development
- granting of credit to the Bank of Commerce and Development
- issuing of bonds.

The Bank of Commerce and Development should be subordinate to the Central Bank and should directly carry out the operations of commercial credit and investment with the rest of the economic subjects in the country. It will also centralise credits with foreign banks. A fundamental role of this bank will be the granting of credit for private and cooperative sectors to encourage their growth, coordinating with general monetary policies. By definition the Bank of Commerce and Development will be a Type A enterprise and will operate with profits from any source.[148]

---

[146]   The low average level of Cuban customs duties (8%), and the absence of significant non-tariff barriers in Cuba, is an advantage for bilateral agreements with other countries in the region.

[147]   The details released about the programme of banking reform that the Cuban government is gradually implementing includes the separation of the Central Bank from the Bank of Commerce and Development.

[148]   When we say that the Bank of Commerce and Development is a Type A enterprise, we do not exclude the existence of more than one firm. There could be a division into a Commercial Bank and a Development Bank. These, in turn, could be subdivided by sectors. But the most important factor is that, because of the importance of the Bank in economic development, they should be Type A enterprises.

In this phase the expansion of credit should be compatible with the growth of production to achieve a better financial pressure on enterprises driving them towards a more efficient use of available resources. The present situation in which the Bank indirectly finances the losses of state enterprises *via* cancelled credits must cease. The final decision about the closure of enterprises should be taken by the government with the participation of the directors and the Bank of Commerce.

It is not accidental that we have omitted a discussion of the rate of interest which in this phase will play a secondary role in the state sector. In a centralised economic planning system, such as serves as the point of departure for the programme, the rate of interest plays practically no role in the assignment of resources. However, even in this first stage, as financial pressure in the state sector increases, the rate of interest will begin to play a more relevant role in the evaluation of the enterprises' performance. In the case of the private and cooperative sectors, the rate of interest will be used to ration credit. Monetary resources frozen in bank accounts will be used, above the level of annual permitted withdrawals, in order to support investment in the non-state sector.

State investment

In this first stage, because of the shortage of resources, the state will continue to centralise state investment and direct it basically to strategic sectors and generators of exports as well as to the restoration of the physical and social infrastructure.

All this process of reform of the state machinery and state enterprises requires training for the management and state functionaries, for the assemblies of *Poder Popular*, and the Administrative Boards of companies in order to lead to the evolution of the economic system in later stages.

The passage to the second stage will occur when:

– the minimum social and physical infrastructure has been restored in order to allow the state to provide an adequate supply of public goods and services;

– the most dynamic sectors have created their own reproductive base that will gradually allow the market greater freedom in the assignment of excess production;

– the efficiency of state enterprises has improved and the bases for a 'strong' system of financial control for this sector has been achieved.[149]

These three conditions are essential in order to begin the process of the

---

[149]   In Kornai's 'classical' use of the concept 'strong'.

construction of a socialist market.

Stage 2. Transition to a regulated market

The second stage is a transition, characterised by the beginning of the construction of a market for means of production for the state sector. This is the most complex stage of the programme and is crucial for the success of restructuring. Its successful implementation will guarantee the direction of later stages of the reform. Its failure will terminate the programme. It has the following primary objectives:

– to give continuity to the decentralisation of the state sector of the economy, begun in the first stage;

– to initiate the construction of a market for means of production for the state sector, and extend it to other sectors.

The inauguration of the construction of a market for the state sector must be based on a strong system of financial restrictions which will ensure that state enterprises operate under criteria of profitability.

In spite of the introduction and development of competition between state enterprises and in general in other sectors, this stage will be marked by a selective policy in terms of monetary, fiscal and external economic policy which will privilege the activities and firms defined by the industrial policy adopted.

Reform of state enterprises

(a) The enterprises classified as Type A will be subordinated to control by ministries of central government. Those classified as Type B and C will be the responsiblity of the *Poder Popular* assemblies at the appropriate level under the direct control of their Administrative Boards.

b) All enterprises of the state sector can accumulate part of their profits for investment. The proportion of retained profits will be increased according to the level of decentralisation of state investment.

c) A parallel internal market for means of production will be gradually introduced, beginning with those which will have least overall impact on the economy. The planned allocation of material and financial resources (including foreign exchange) to the state entities will be confined to principal necessities and the market will play a growing role until it has reached the desired equilibrium.

The principal sources for the construction of this market in means of production, to which all economic agents will have access, will be:

– the sale of surpluses generated by enterprises, after fulfilling planned targets;

– the free sale of imported means of production after planned distribution has been carried out;

– the sale of foreign exchange according to the procedures explained in the relevant paragraph about exchange policy in the second stage;

– supply from non-state enterprises – in order to link state enterprises with the non-state sector *via* the market the former need to be under strict financial control.

d) Non-profitable enterprises must be closed, other than those for which the government has fixed explicit subsidies, because of their situation as nascent or strategic industries or because their closure will present serious social problems.[150]

e) The government will determine production targets for supplies from state enterprises (basic supplies)[151] and leave a space for inter-enterprise coordination for the determination of the remaining supplies and quantities. During this stage the proportion of directed supply will be gradually reduced. State contracts, both for state enterprises and others, will tend to give price advantages, when this is necessary, encouraging tendering for these.

Re-articulation of other forms of ownership

The measures started in the first stage will be continued. The market for means of production regulated by the state will be extended, and non-state enterprises will also have access to it. Commercial relations between the state and non-state sectors will be increased.

In this stage firms of professionals (accountants, consultants, and software designers etc) will play a more active role. On the other hand, there will have been an increase in the concentration of private or cooperative ownership up to

---

[150] During the process of gradual liberalisation of prices it is necessary to take into account that even prices fixed by the state must be revised to incorporate modifications in liberated prices. If this is not taken into account artificial losses or unwarranted profits could be generated. The closure of an enterprise is a very complex process and must take into account technical criteria such as the analysis of relative costs, defined as future costs which will be incurred according to different alternatives under consideration. Its evaluation is important for decisions relative to closure of lines of production, replacement of equipment and rent or purchase of means of production. On occasion, in the light of analysis of relevant costs, it is preferable to maintain the production of supplies or services which are loss-making with respect to total costs. See Hangren (1976).

[151] In principle the state will maintain the power to determine levels of supplies of important essentials for the development programme, so that neither the 'pure' market nor methods of indirect regulation will govern their production, which would in this case suffer from lack of regularity.

the limits fixed in the first stage, which can be revised at any point.

Social Security

The same policy begun in the first stage will be continued. The reduction in the pressure on compensatory mechanisms of social security is envisaged to the extent of any improvement in production, and levels of employment. Minimum income levels that are the basis for compensatory transfer payments to vulnerable groups will be revised.

Wage and Prices Policy

In this stage there will be important changes in this area:

a) Gradual liberalisation of prices of means of production in the state sector that are not included in state planning (beginning with those sectors with relatively less impact on the economy). However, this liberalisation is likely to be closely followed by the oligopolisation or monopolisation of a large part of this market. The discretionary action of the state will impose maximum levels for all prices, avoiding an inflationary spiral. The control of prices of products that are crucial to political and social stability will be maintained.

b) The non-free prices (basically those of Type A enterprises) must include the modifications which are occurring in free price markets in order not to provoke reverses in the updating of the non-free prices.

c) Continuation of the consumer price policies started in the first stage.

d) Discretionary control of prices in the farmers' markets and for goods produced by the non-state sector of the economy.

e) Liberalisation of wages of decentralised state enterprises, with preference for the adoption of participatory wage systems. In order to avoid abrupt changes it is important that prices and wages are near to equilibrium[152] at the beginning of this phase. Once they are liberated, it is important to synchronise wage increases in decentralised enterprises with those in centralised and directly controlled entities to avoid negative tensions.

f) In this whole process of freeing wage levels the state must be cautious so as to avoid severe inflationary shocks. This might extend to the establishment of wage control during certain periods.

g) A minimum wage will be fixed for the private and cooperative sectors. By this stage more stability and concentration should have come about in this sector

---

[152]   This is also true for the exchange rate.

making it easier to control.

Exchange Policy

In developing countries without a complete productive structure and where there are many bottlenecks, internal levels of inflation often exceed those in industrialised countries. In these conditions a system of periodic mini-devaluations is common, but in all cases it is essential to ensure that the exchange rate is not over-valued; it is more appropriate to have a neutral or pro-export exchange rate. In the context of this proposal, Cuba should adjust the exchange rate according to the factors outlined above.

During this stage monetary dualism in domestic transactions of state enterprises will be gradually reduced – those participating in self-financing schemes and those which receive a direct allocation of foreign exchange and also in the transactions of foreign firms within the country. By the end of this stage, to the extent that the market has consolidated and reserves of foreign exchange have accumulated, conditions will be created for the total elimination of monetary dualism.

The partial convertibility of the Cuban peso will be established. In the context of economic growth in which the proportion of directly allocated resources including foreign exchange is reduced, the relative availability of these resources for distribution to economic agents *via* market mechanisms will be increased. This will make possible the gradual initiation of the sale of foreign exchange to state sector enterprises, but not for use within the domestic economy, and with precise control of exchange rates, prioritising the targets for investment. Also individuals and the non-state sector will be able to buy foreign exchange, but under strong regulation to avoid capital flight.

The coordination of exchange policy with monetary and fiscal policy is central for the inauguration and development of the convertibility of the peso (See Annex 5).

Budget

The line adopted in the first stage will be continued and some measures already announced will be consolidated:

a) Deepening the reform of state machinery, through the decentralisation of enterprise activities and the new functions that the government will assume.

b) Deepening taxation reform *via* the introduction of organisational, institutional and fiscal conditions which will prevent tax evasion. The new tax system must be applied in a gradual manner to state enterprises, leaving part of their profits for future investment.

The new tax system should also be gradually applied to private and cooperative firms. Taxes on wages and property will play a central role in the creation of a progressive tax system.

Value Added Tax (VAT) could be an effective tax to substitute for taxes on specific sales. The possibility of exemptions on specified basic consumer items will make this a progressive tax. However, it is important to take into account the note of caution introduced previously in Chapter 3. Fixed taxes for non-state enterprises will be applied only when the small scale of production and commercialisation prevents a true declaration of profits. The creation of a legal and regulatory framework is the *sine qua non* for the success of restructuring. Accounting firms (state or non-state) will play an important role in this stage.

The taxation structure will depend, from the quantitative point of view, on various factors that should be considered together:

– the international tax structure (in order not to discourage foreign investment or affect competition from national entities);

– the size of public expenditure;

– the level of equity which must be achieved at any given moment;

– macroeconomic conditions and problems requiring immediate solution: inflation, employment and growth in investment;

– the stimulation of certain sectors and specific enterprises.

c) Subsidies which are considered necessary to maintain certain state enterprises can be authorised by the state. A bankruptcy law will be established for state sector enterprises.

d) A greater degree of autonomy for local governments in executing their budgets. The resources from state and non-state sector enterprises, and part of income and property taxes from the population, will be the main source to meet expenditure. The areas in which local government will assume control of financing of activities will be defined.

e) It is of utmost importance to maintain a fiscal balance or a manageable deficit to avoid inflationary shocks or pressures on the balance of payments. All this implies the coordination of monetary policy with foreign trade policy.

Foreign trade

a) At the beginning, the scheme of self-financing and the current system of allocation of foreign exchange must be maintained according to planned limits. As we pointed out above, as this stage proceeds the market will assume a greater importance and consequently the role of administrative mechanisms will be reduced. Gradually the sale of foreign exchange to enterprises requiring foreign purchases will increase.

b) Tariffs will play an important role in the improvement of distributional efficiency. Their gradual reduction will be carried out following proper notice, and will be coordinated with national enterprises according to agreement determined by the state's industrial policy.

c) Another mechanism will be the determination of import quotas for certain products which will include the allocations of quotas in coordination with industrial policy.

d) Subsidies will be maintained for strategic production, nascent industries or those whose sudden closure would have negative social impact.

e) Import duties will continue to play a key role in international negotiations.

f) Plant hygiene and environmental norms will be applied.

g) The opening of trade will have to align specific national interests with obligations which are contracted internationally.

Banking: Monetary and credit policy

The Central Bank must define monetary and credit policy. In this stage the expansion of credit started at the end of the last phase will continue.

The Bank of Commerce and Development must extend financing to investments of state enterprises, according to the interests of the state in certain sectors, and according to the economic need of the enterprises. Rates of interest must be differentiated according to sectors and regions. This policy will be extended to the cooperative and private sectors.

During the second stage a central aspect of the economic policy in this area will be institution-building – that is, the implanting and improving of a range of organisational and normative modifications which will define with clarity and predictability monetary policy and the management of credit and the interest rate.

Another important task of economic policy in this area will be the progressive introduction of new financial instruments and intermediate financial institutions which it is decided to utilise, and which will be consolidated in the third stage (for example, the creation of a market for state capital for the expansion or creation of decentralised enterprises.)

State investment

Initially the policy of centralisation of investment must be continued, but gradually a growing part of investment can be carried out in a decentralised manner by state enterprises financed by their own funds or by bank credit. In this context of greater decentralisation the state will hold the initiative and control, and will be a major factor in the investment process.

Stage 3: Decentralisation of the Economy

The third stage will begin when, on the one hand, the management of state enterprises has been strengthened, and, on the other, when there are real possibilities for the increase in the scale of the markets for means of production and foreign exchange.

This third stage consists of the construction of the model of normal functioning of the economy. The government retains great power in the execution of economic policy, which it can exercise discretionally, and at the same time there is widespread decentralisation of management of state sector enterprises which coexist with diverse forms of ownership and economic organisation.

The objective of the new model is the application of a system of relations between all economic subjects in society in such a way that political power will remain in the hands of the people and, at the same time, the greatest potential of the economy will be developed on the basis of social justice.

The application of industrial policy will take place through the use of economic instruments by the state, at the same time as indirect instruments will begin to play a more active role.

Reform of state enterprise

a) Direct planning by the government will be limited to the centralised enterprises and other basic supplies from decentralised state, private and cooperative enterprises. The economic directives in the plan will have the character of law and must be approved annually by the National Assembly of *Poder Popular*. The most appropriate institutional mechanism must be adopted to ensure the participation of the social organisations and other levels of *Poder Popular* (national, provincial, municipal) in the formulation, revision and approval of the *'plan directivo'* of the national economy. For the non-centralised enterprises (state and non-state) the government will utilise mechanisms to stimulate signing of contracts, including encouraging tenders.

b) The market for means of production will become a normal mechanism for obtaining these goods for state and non-state enterprises. Prices will be fixed according to supply and demand except in the cases where price ceilings are imposed.

c) Normally the state enterprises will finance their investments totally from profits or other funds of their own, or from bank credits and sales of shares. The central government, however, can finance risky investments as a joint venture with such firms, including those in the private or cooperative sector.

Rearticulation of other forms of ownership

All economic sectors (state, cooperative, private or individual) will be integrated in the same market so that they are mutually complementary. The only significant differences will be determined by the general limits established for the growth of private agents and the delimitation of areas reserved for state investment. Other forms of preferential treatment which could be used will not depend on the form of ownership but the sector or the activity in which they operate, according to industrial policy.

Social security

The trend towards employment growth must be continued. In addition to macroeconomic instruments, the state will have the power to manage centrally productive investment directed towards employment generation.

The minimum wage, like the policy of giving subsidies to people whose income is below the minimum wage, will be linked to the general growth in wages and will be under continuous review. No person will be left without social protection. The policy of social security will be coordinated with the freeing of wages discussed below.

Price and wage policy

a) The government must regulate prices to avoid monopoly and oligopoly prices.

b) The prices of means of production in all sectors, state and non-state, will be set by the market except where the state imposes price ceilings or fixes prices.

c) In this stage generalised rationing of consumer goods will be eliminated, and as a principle prices will be set by supply and demand. This will not preclude the state setting maximum prices.

d) The freeing of wages will be maintained in decentralised state enterprises. The government will retain the power to impose wage controls for brief periods to counteract surges of inflationary pressure.

Exchange rate policy

A single exchange rate will be retained for economic transactions within the country, which will be either neutral or biased towards export and which can be modified by means of mini-devaluations at standard intervals to avoid the overvaluation of the national currency.[153]

A broad-based convertibility of the Cuban peso will be established for activities related to the current account of the balance of payments. The convertibility will be flexible for individuals and non-state enterprises. In the state sector the schemes of self-financing and direct assignment of foreign exchange will be discontinued, so that all state enterprises will have to meet their foreign exchange requirements *via* direct exchange. There will be established convertibility guarantees for foreign investment, compatible with other policies in this area. In all cases there will be precise exchange controls, particularly for transactions on the capital account and for certain products and activities in the current account.

Monetary dualism will be virtually eliminated as practically all operations within the country will be carried out in national currency.

Budget

The policies adopted in the previous stage will be continued in the sense of guaranteeing adequate levels of social expenditure, improvements to the taxation system and the avoidance of dangerous deficits. Fiscal policy will be converted into a strong tool for macroeconomic planning in order to achieve growth in production and employment and to avoid high levels of inflation. Also, microeconomic policy will play a strong role in the stimulation of specific sectors, enterprises and regions.

Foreign trade

Trade policy will continue to play a fundamental role in the global efficiency of the economy, given the importance of foreign trade and the growing liberalisation of trade promoted by the Cuban government which predates a restructuring programme such as is proposed here.

The state will maintain its ability to intervene within this more open trade context, in order to protect the economic, social and political interests of the country. This will require the utilisation of the whole range of mechanisms (tariff and non-tariff) with the objective of protecting nascent industries in dynamic

---

[153] There has been a vigorous debate within the academic world about whether the exchange rate should be fixed or flexible. The selection of an 'adjustable' fixed rate for this third stage is derived from the authors' interpretation of the predictions for the Cuban economy under the plans proposed. Even in this stage, in spite of higher distributional efficiency associated with a single rate, it may be considered appropriate to use a different rate for tourists, as in the previous stage. This will be determined by the necessity to raise the internal rate of saving, and therefore the prices of certain consumer goods may be relatively high for a prolonged period.

sectors and other sectors which are strategic in social terms. However, as a principle trade policy should be geared to enabling the country to produce either what is determined by comparative advantage or what is strategic for its security.

Also, special attention will be given to the functioning of the national economy under the principle of the norms of international trade that are adopted – whether multilateral, regional or bilateral. This will require both that Cuba respects these principles and also that international dispute settlement procedures are applied.

Banking: monetary and credit policy

The Central Bank will retain two powerful tools: control of monetary and exchange policy. It will aim to achieve a sustained increase in production and employment, control of inflation and equilibrium in the balance of payments.

The Bank of Commerce and Development will play a central role in the development of the sectors and activities determined by state planning. A relatively wide range of financial instruments will operate as well as such non-bank intermediary financial institutions as may be decided should be used. The regulated markets for state capital will extend the mobility of investment and the diversification and linkages of state enterprises.

State investment

The government will maintain the capacity to invest directly in enterprises it administers in new spheres or in others in which they compete with decentralised entities (state or non-state). It can also decide whether to decentralise enterprises created by such investment.

The investment policy of the government will play a key role in the implementation of macroeconomic planning. Decentralised state enterprises will direct their investments according to market signals, with corrective intervention by specific government action as appropriate.

CHAPTER 5

Postscript. The demonetisation of the Cuban economy: A review of the alternatives

Demonetisation: A problem resolved?

In March 1996, twenty-one months after the rationalisation of internal finances, it is clear that excess liquidity is still a problem awaiting a solution. The gradual demonetisation of the economy adopted in May 1994 has achieved relatively modest results, with high levels of accumulated liquidity still remaining and with a marked tendency towards strong levels of concentration. In fact, we can see decreasing effectiveness of the instruments employed in the first year and a half of the programme.

In our view it is necessary to proceed with a significant reduction in the level of liquidity as one of the necessary conditions to consolidate the reactivation of the national economy; this will inevitably require new measures. We are aware that this is not a view shared by all specialists, so that before we proceed further it is important to spell out our own position concerning the real nature of the problem of excess liquidity in the Cuban economy at the beginning of 1996.

Some new interpretations take the view that the measures adopted have basically resolved the problems that existed a year ago, reducing them to a 'manageable' level, even when the official figure of total liquidity of 9,100 million pesos exceeds by almost three times the level considered as an equilibrium one.[154]

This view recognises the high degree of contraction of circulation, but emphasises that 60% of this money is deposited in accounts which 'have a very low level of movement' and thus 'do not constitute a real pressure factor in the current economy'. It is worth pointing out, however, that the most recent tendencies appear to contradict the supposed immobility of these bank deposits. According to the *Informe Económico* (August 1995), although there was a reduction of ordinary savings of only 147 million pesos in the whole of 1994, there was a further reduction of 451 million in the first six months of 1995, which could imply a total reduction of approximately 1,000 million in 1995.

---

[154] The necessary money supply was estimated by the government as 3,500 pesos (figures from *Granma*, 'Granma entrevista a José Luis Rodríguez, Ministro de Finanzas y Precios', Havana, 22 November 1994). The required level of money supply in circulation depends on the concrete conditions of the economy. Although we do not know the basis on which this official estimate was based, the subsequent structural transformations undergone by the Cuban economy, which have had repercussions on the level of prices, on supply and certainly on the velocity of circulation of money – and also the liquidating of a large percentage of deposits – must have changed this level.

Nor does this analysis recognise the other dimension of this issue, the fall in income levels, since this is viewed as amenable to manipulation by taxation policy. From this perspective it makes little sense to take on the costs and risks implied by acting on the excess liquidity problem which 'in fact does not exist as a problem at this moment'.

In our view this is an interpretation which ignores other dimensions of the problem which we consider require solution as part of the process of an integrated restructuring of the Cuban economy.

There is evidence that excess liquidity and its concentration continue to exert strong pressure on the economy as a whole, especially in the new markets which are being created. The high level of prices in the farmers' markets and their relative rigidity after a year of operation cannot be solely or chiefly explained as a problem of inadequate supply. In our view one of the central causes of the phenomenon is the persistence of a high and concentrated level of monetary overhang (including bank deposits) which exerts considerable inflationary pressure on the economy.

The level of prices (especially in the farmers' markets) maintains a disproportionate relationship with the average level of wages in the country, which produces rigidities in the structure of individual consumption,[155] constrains the possibilities of restoring a situation in which the wage is a fundamental source of income, and creates a series of complex problems for the national economy. Amongst the most important are: (a) distortions in agrarian production as a consequence of the different levels of profitability derived from activities linked to the regulated and the unregulated market; (b) the relative stagnation of activity in those areas of legalised free market activity which are not agrarian; (c) the lack of incentives for peasant producers and some cooperatives who still have a high level of savings in national currency with no appropriate supply of goods; and (d) the high level of transfer of resources from the city to the countryside.

Finally, beyond the discussion of the real pressure imposed by excess liquidity, including bank deposits, at this moment, is the central question of its impact on the subsequent process of restructuring. Decentralisation and the greater diversification of forms of ownership and organisation of production and services is in our view an inevitable feature of the immediate future in order to raise the level of efficiency in the state sector and to alleviate the employment problem.

However, the ongoing problem of excess and concentrated liquidity can at any moment have an adverse effect, not only from the economic perspective, but

---

[155]   A significant part of the urban population has to deploy the greater part of its wage in the free market as a necessary complement to the rationed goods obtained in the regulated market.

also from the political point of view. Therefore, we consider that it is extremely relevant to re-evaluate the problem of accumulated liquidity, both for the present and for the future. It is appropriate, therefore, to examine the possible alternatives.

The present chapter is aimed at reevaluating these alternatives, from a broad economic, social and political framework, given that the monetary overhang is a process which, by its very nature, goes beyond the strictly economic sphere.

We consider it essential, as a conceptual premise in order to articulate an effective 'demonetisation' programme in Cuba, to have an economic programme that transcends the monetary-financial domain. In fact, this consideration was implicit in the debates which preceded the adoption of the present demonetisation plan. However, it is clear that its implementation has proceeded in a way which is not clearly linked to any specifically formulated integrated economic programme. The simultaneous existence of actions in other areas of the economy indicates that the changes have been relatively broad, but this does not mean that they are necessarily part of a properly integrated programme of transformation.

Without doubt the failure to link the process of demonetisation within an integrated programme of changes limits the possibility of evaluating it and can lead to the adoption of a narrow focus centred on the analysis of basic monetary, financial and 'technical' short-term parameters.

The limitations pointed out could be resolved by considering demonetisation in a larger context. Here it is important to emphasise the existence of two levels in the analysis: first, the evaluation of the process as it is, and as it has come about in relation to other real changes, and secondly a comparative study of the process of demonetisation that has taken place, taking as a reference point an integrated model of economic transformation.

The importance of the first level is clearly that it permits a perspective on the economy as a system; the second level is important because it leads to considering alternatives as part of an integrated programme. In the analysis which follows we have tried to consider the programme of gradual demonetisation in relation to other changes, particularly those associated with the opening of the market, and the development of a non-state sector of the economy. On the other hand, the integrated model of economic transformation taken as the reference point is the one proposed by the authors in the first edition of this book,[156] and which has been fundamentally developed in Chapters 3 and 4 of the present edition. We could have chosen a different model, but preferred to adopt a model which has already been disseminated at national level.

In the following pages we examine the theme of alternatives to

---

[156] See 1995 edition.

demonetisation in the following manner: first, we give some details of the current programme, particularly in relation to the debate which took place at the end of 1993 and the beginning of 1994 about currency substitution. Secondly, we give a description and brief evaluation of the programme of gradual demonetisation adopted in May 1994, indicating its principal effects. Thirdly, we evaluate the main alternatives to continuing this policy. And finally we propose some considerations which the authors consider would be the most appropriate approach to the problem of demonetisation, given the current conditions in Cuba.

Background to the Demonetisation Programme of 1994

The adjustment programme carried out in Cuba at the beginning of the 1990s had specific characteristics which distinguished it from adjustment programmes adopted in other countries. The impact on consumption and investment levels was much higher than in other countries, but the main distinguishing characteristic was the equitable distribution of the costs of the crisis, and the maintenance of basic social services with universal access for the Cuban population.

The specificity of the Cuban adjustment was determined to a large extent by the depth of the crisis, the unpredictability of its immediate impact, the initial perception of its transitory nature, and most importantly the objectives of equity and social justice of the Cuban Revolution.

Rationing of basic consumer goods was a principal element of the Cuban adjustment policy adopted in the face of the reduction in levels of supply, as well as fixing prices at levels which everybody could afford, the maintenance of employment by means of subsidies to enterprises, and important social programmes such as health, education and social security, all of which had a considerable impact on maintaining political consensus even in the most difficult economic conditions. Of course, there were costs which became heavier as the crisis continued and became more acute, and particularly when it became clear that it was not a transitory phenomenon.

Excess money supply was possibly the most 'visible' cost of this adjustment programme. Although at the beginning of the process the recovery of production was seen as a solution to the crisis, by the end of 1993 it was realised that the financial disequilibria had reached a level which prevented any successful reactivation of the economy. The most notable effects of excess liquidity were: (a) increased indiscipline in the work force and the reduction of the intensity of work in the state sector; (b) the growth of the '*submerged* economy' and the consequent re-location of labour to activities of lower social priority and real productivity to the detriment of key sectors; (c) the inflationary process of the *submerged* market to which people had to resort with increasing frequency both as sellers and buyers; and (d) the loss of value of the national currency and therefore of the wage, which had adverse effects not only in the economic sphere but also in the political and ideological spheres.[157]

By the end of 1993 two principal options for confronting this situation were considered: (a) the exchange of the national currency, with the confiscation or 'freezing' of a large part of the accumulated cash; and (b) a programme of gradual demonetisation which would lead to an acceptable level of liquidity. In fact the second session of the National Assembly of *Poder Popular* in December 1993 initiated a wide debate in all work centres throughout the country about economic issues, in particular the rationalisation of domestic finances, culminating in the Extraordinary Session of the National Assembly of *Poder Popular* in May 1994, when it was decided to adopt the second option, i.e. a process of gradual demonetisation of the economy.

The arguments against the currency replacement option included the direct economic cost involved in substituting the national currency, especially given the critical situation with regard to access to foreign exchange which affected the whole country. But this reason was rapidly discarded in the extraordinary parliamentary session of May 1994, on the basis that the cost was not as high as had been assumed and that, in the last instance, if this was the appropriate option then the costs should be faced.[158]

Another argument was that the population would lose confidence in the National Bank if there was a currency replacement accompanied by some form of confiscation, or by measures equivalent to a quasi-confiscation, such as freezing accounts. This concern was valid in general, although in practice there are ways of implementing a limited currency replacement accompanied by confiscation which takes care to minimise if not eliminate its possible negative impact on public confidence in the National Bank. However, while it is true that certain minority sectors of the population (those which held the major part of the liquid assets) envisaged that they would be affected by partial confiscation of their bank accounts, this cannot be identified as a factor which would generate widespread lack of confidence in the banking system.[159]

The preoccupation with the possible undermining of confidence in the banking system would have had more weight if the planned partial confiscation had involved only money in bank accounts, but since it dealt with the substitution of all cash regardless of where it was deposited, this argument lost some of its validity. It would even be possible to have a different treatment of money deposited in bank accounts which would have *improved* confidence in the banking system.

---

[157] See Carranza Valdés (1994).
[158] See *Granma*, 'Finalizó el 11 período ordinario de sesiones de la Asamblea', 29 December 1993.
[159] In December 1994 86% of savings accounts had balances of less than 2,000 pesos, which is a level which could be easily protected during a currency substitution, especially taking into account that these accounts only represented 22.2% of the ordinary savings of the population.

Another reason which was explicitly mentioned in both sessions of the Assembly (December 1993 and May 1994), and which was, in our view, the decisive factor, was the danger that excess liquidity would reappear after the currency replacement.[160] In the context of the incomplete economic programme which was subsequently approved it was implicit that it was preferable to avoid a measure which would be potentially problematic in political terms,[161] and whose effects were not totally predictable in the medium and long term. However, this left open the possibility that a currency substitution could be carried out at a later date if this became necessary.

Of course, such a perception was logical in the absence of an integrated programme of structural economic transformation which would minimise from the outset the probability of repeating the problem of excess liquidity by modifying the causal factors. A substitution which was isolated or which was part of an inadequately articulated reform programme would be condemned *ex ante* to failure, and at best would only offer temporary relief offset by negative long-term political and economic consequences. Currency substitution directly hurts the property rights of those affected, and requires as an indispensable condition that it is part of an integral programme of measures to facilitate the establishment of favourable political conditions and ensure their acceptance and support among the majority of the population.

The option of gradual demonetisation of the economy adopted in May 1994 represented in practice – beyond its intentions and partial successes – the postponement of the establishment of functional levels of monetary equilibrium and the need to confront the consequences of the concentration of liquidity, objectives which in our view should be achieved at the start of any programme of economic restructuring of the Cuban economy. With hindsight, it is clear that the decision depended not so much on the intrinsic merits of the option selected but on the uncertainty which was associated with the more radical alternative of a currency substitution and subsequent economic changes.

---

[160]   See *Granma*, 'Finalizó el 11 período ordinario de sessiones de la Asamblea', 29 December 1993, and *Granma*, 'Reseña de los debates de la primera jornada', 2 May 1994. An element which appears to have had some weight in this perception is the existence of various negative international experiences, such as that of Vietnam in the 1980s, when a currency replacement did not lead to the expected results. However, a rigorous analysis of these experiences indicates that the problem consisted in the lack of connection between the substitution and the rest of the reform programme which should have modified the causes of the initial excess liquidity.

[161]   The political problems which could have followed from a currency substitution at the beginning of 1994 can be identified at two levels. On the one hand, the possibility of rejection by certain social sectors at a time when the maintenance of political consensus was a priority; and, on the other, the negative reaction of private agricultural producers in the short term. This could have led to a reduction in supply at a time when food supplies had fallen to critical levels, although it should be borne in mind that this could have been mitigated by specific measures as part of the substitution. However, in our view the most important point is that the vast majority of the population apparently did not strongly oppose a currency replacement in early and mid-1994.

The Programme of Gradual Demonetisation

The programme of gradual reduction of excess liquidity put in place in mid-1994 comprised principally the following measures: increase in the prices of a raft of consumer goods and services; abolition of certain free services without affecting what are considered as the basic achievements of the Revolution in social terms; application of a new taxation law; changes in the policy of subsidies to state enterprises; and tighter requirements and controls to restore financial discipline in the state sector.[162]

The greater burden of the programme rests on the price increases, particularly of tobacco products and alcohol.[163] These measures resulted in a 16% reduction in circulation between May and December 1994, but in 1995 the process slowed down and only achieved a fall of 7% in the first 9 months of that year.[164] In September 1995 money in circulation, estimated at 9,100 million pesos, already represented 2.6 times the equilibrium level of liquidity according to government calculations,[165] leading to the paradoxical situation, which we have already noted, of the existence of an excess liquidity according to official calculations, whilst for the large part of the domestic economy what was being extracted was not 'excess' but 'necessary' liquidity.

The extraction of surplus cash has been a double process: on the one hand, it has reduced the total amount of cash in circulation, and on the other it has generated a larger concentration of *passive liquidity*,[166] which carries the implicit danger that it will be converted into *active liquidity* and unleash greater inflationary pressures in the face of the creation of new market opportunities.[167]

---

[162]   See Carranza Valdés (1994).

[163]   81.2% of the reduction in excess liquidity up to November 1994 corresponded to the increase in prices and liberalisation of sales of cigars and alcoholic beverages. See *Granma*, 'Intervención de José Luis Rodríguez. Presentación del Proyecto de Ley de Presupuesto para el año 1995', 21 December 1994.

[164]   Calculation from *La economía cubana en 1994*, Oficina Nacional de Estadísticas, June 1995; and *Granma*, 'Confiamos en quienes no se dejaron doblegar por las presiones e invirtieron en Cuba: mañana serán más', 27 October 1995.

[165]   This refers to the level of 3,500 million pesos cited above, about which we have previously introduced a note of caution.

[166]   This includes not only cash deposited in bank accounts, but also cash in the hands of the population (held for precautionary reasons). Although there are no data available to indicate accurately the structure of concentration of total liquidity, there is one part of the total whose distribution it is possible to discern: ordinary savings. The *Informe Económico* of the Banco Nacional de Cuba (August 1995) acknowledged that in the period December 1994 - June 1995 there was a high concentration of deposits in a small number of accounts. In June 1995 13.6% of savings accounts accounted for 82.4% of the value of deposits. Taking into account that ordinary savings represented in June 1995 64% of accumulated liquidity, this a general indication of the increased overall concentration.

[167]   Although we will return to this point later, it is useful to clarify from the beginning our criteria by which *passive liquidity* represents an economic problem which should not be minimised: first, because it explains to a large extent the inflationary pressures that determine price levels in the free markets and which do not retain any rational relation with average income levels. These prices,

The programme of demonetisation which has been implemented appears to have arrived at its two limits; on the one hand, the size of active liquidity, according to the empirical data available, appears to have reached the quantity of money necessary for commercial transactions and, on the other, the possibilities that the population can continue to act as the principal 'source' of extraction have been exhausted, in the context of a programme of demonetisation based on increases in prices of basic consumer goods. To this extent the programme has resolved part of the problem (limited reduction in liquidity), but has left unresolved the achievement of more appropriate levels of money in circulation while also reinforcing the concentration of money holdings.[168]

The experience of the programme so far indicates that its principal characteristic has been not so much the achievement of gradual demonetisation but rather a regressive programme in terms of the concentration of its effects on those groups with lower levels of liquidity and income. The first aspect explains the permanency of the imbalances, in spite of the time which has elapsed; the second leads to the complication of the possible alternative solutions, above all because it has been produced in the context of the opening of larger parts of the market, and the growth of the private and cooperative sectors.[169] This has

---

after an initial period of reduction, have been maintained at high levels in relation to average wages. The fact that there are limitations of supply in these markets cannot in itself explain the high prices. Secondly, there are no rigid barriers between *active* and *passive* liquidity; in fact, in 1994 and 1995 the fluctuations in savings accounts have represented an increasing source of active liquidity. Thirdly, the high level of concentration of accumulated liquidity represents an important barrier to the necessary enlargement of non-state markets and is very questionable from a socialist perspective. This last point makes very clear the need to integrate the process of demonetisation with other components of a larger programme of economic transformation.

[168]   Of course, this is not necessarily a negative effect for those who support the reestablishment of a market economy in Cuba, to the extent that this concentration of money is perceived as a legitimate and desirable source of original capital accumulation. However, in the wide range of works published abroad there appear to be different positions on this issue. For some analysts, such as Juan Luis Moreno, any form of expropriation of liquidity is an attack on the informal sectors, which are basic to the capitalist reconstruction; Jorge A. Sanguinetty questions the existence of excess liquidity and considers it 'involuntary savings'. Other authors, such as Pastor and Zimbalist, who have distanced themselves from traditional formulae for the reestablishment of a market economy in Cuba, consider it necessary to take advantage of the entrepreneurial capacity attributed to 'black market operators'. Curiously, some authors, such as Montalván and Castañeda, who explicitly support the reestablishment of capitalism in Cuba, propose measures which represent a quasi-confiscation. This point illustrates that the debate on demonetisation derives not only from ideological considerations, but also from technical premises. See Moreno (1993); Sanguinetty (1991); Pastor and Zimbalist (1995); and Castañeda and Montalván (1993a, 1993b).

[169]   The opening of the farmers' markets on 1 October 1994 and the extension of the presence of the private and cooperative sectors, after the initiation of the demonetisation programme but in the presence of a high level of monetary concentration, have represented in practice a huge process of monetary legitimisation. On the one hand, this has led to a state of *de facto* economic amnesty which favours those social sectors which for a long time operated in non-legal spaces, complicating the already existing difficult problems associated with the development of differentiated income and savings distribution in a socialist society. On the other hand, the phenomenon complicates the perception of the legitimacy of accumulated liquidity, a problem which makes it difficult if not impossible to apply partially confiscatory measures and in effect limits the options available for financial rationalisation. It should be stressed that the opinion just expressed does not in any way

favoured the legal concentration of income in those very social sectors which were already accumulating cash, largely illegally, before the beginning of the programme.

The demonetisation of the economy is, as we have already said, a relevant and topical issue. In the case of Cuba in particular it is linked to a socialist restructuring, which gives it greater significance than it might have in other countries in transition to 'market economies' or which carry out macroeconomic stabilisation plans of a neo-liberal type.[170]

In our view, demonetisation is not solely a necessary condition from the technical point of view for a profound re-structuring of the economy, but it is also above all a political problem on whose solution depends to a good measure the progress of the restructuring process and its ultimate coherence.

In Chapter 4 we detailed the possible negative consequences of a process of gradual demonetisation on the basis of the conditions of the Cuban economy. Below we briefly review these negative consequences, trying to adjust them to current conditions.

The political effect. When it was decided in mid-1994 to implement the programme of gradual demonetisation, the point of departure was a very high concentration of liquidity.[171] Illegal sources had contributed to accumulation in the submerged economy, and 'legal' sources were in large measure the result of distortions in the market from eras before the current crisis, and which allowed for the securing of 'unearned income'. This does not constitute, as has been frequently suggested, a product of entrepreneurial spirit or of 'honest work'.[172] In such circumstances, favourable conditions existed to have carried out a process of confiscation of part of the surplus directed precisely at those principal sectors where such liquidity is concentrated.[173]

It was predictable that a demonetisation programme based on indirect taxes

---

indicate opposition, on the part of the authors of this book, to the necessary opening of markets and non-state economic spaces. What is meant is that these structural changes must be integrated with actions such as financial rationalisation in a single process in which the sequentiality of the measures is crucial in order to produce a favourable economic and political outcome.

[170] That is, to achieve functional levels in determined economic variables, including monetary and financial variables, to ensure the adequate operation of the economic system. The authors do not share other conceptions which give excessive weight to monetary-financial adjustment and which bestow a series of almost 'magic' virtues on equilibrium in these spheres.

[171] There had also been a redistribution of wealth of which liquidity is only one part. But this is not a justification not to act on that part which could be modified and which is also relevant from the point of view of the functioning of the economy in the present context.

[172] For a discussion, see Annex 4, *Repressed Inflation*.

[173] Decree Law 149, May 1994, 'On confiscation of goods and incomes obtained by improper enrichment', was insufficient to identify and confiscate illegal accumulations of wealth. The extension of the market and the private sector makes its future application even more conflictive and diffused.

(*via* prices) would be regressive, since it fell asymmetrically on wide sectors of the population which did not hold the concentrated surpluses. In practice the kind of measures applied, in the context of the extension of markets and the private sector, facilitated the legitimation of money holding and the capitalisation of productive physical assets.

The preservation of monetary accumulations not linked to work and the regressive nature of the financial rationalisation programme represent a political problem in the context of a changing society that has not renounced the important principles of the previous system, such as social justice and the consideration of work as the fundamental source of wealth. The problem is that 'winners' and 'losers' vary from day to day without there ever having been a wide discussion about previous and current paradigms.

In the context of a society in which differentiated economic interests begin to play a more active and open role, it is inevitable that the political question will be asked: who should be affected? In our view such a decision can only be satisfactory if it is the result of a process of debate and consultation in which the majority play a central role and where economic problems are also considered from a political perspective.

The effect on the concentration of money. It was also predictable that the way in which the absolute reduction in total accumulation was carried out, in the conditions of opening of markets and greater presence of private agents,[174] should lead to a higher concentration not only of already existing surplus liquidity but also of income. The phenomenon was particularly worrying given the presence of a weak progressive taxation policy and the reduced redistributive capacity of the state. This has made it ever more difficult to proceed with the demonetisation in the preferred manner[175] and this has had implications for the development of an internal market, which we explain below.

The recessive effect. This is one of the least discussed effects of demonetisation, but it is relevant by virtue of the necessary coherence which recent economic transformations should have. The supply-side measures (increase in own-account work, opening of farmers' markets, industrial and handicraft markets, reforms in the operation of state enterprises) have created favourable conditions for increasing production and employment in the non-state sector. However, the very process of gradual demonetisation itself, in that it constitutes a reduction in aggregate demand and has contributed to the concentration of

---

[174] Privatisation in its widest sense goes beyond the sale of state assets. It also includes the removal of barriers of entry to the private sector, administration contracts, concessions and subcontracting of services previously supplied by the state etc. See Gutiérrez (1994).

[175] For example, the raising of indirect taxes on cigars, tobacco and alcoholic beverages, in the current conditions, will not guarantee a progressive impact on the reduction of liquidity, but rather the opposite.

income, has recessive effects which partially cancel out the supply incentives.[176] At the moment there is a certain stagnation in various non-state activities, especially those which produce goods whose demand is more elastic[177] and in regions of the country where average incomes are low, or where there are no significant inflows of foreign exchange.

The kind of demonetisation programme implemented has created various obstacles to the expansion of aggregate demand. This has created constraints on the growth of self-employment and thus for the rationalisation of the labour force in the state sector.

Market distortions. Gradual demonetisation in conditions of increasing opening of markets and spaces for the non-state sector has had a distortionary effect on the emerging markets, and created new problems for economic policy. The distortions have been particularly acute in the functioning of existing markets for agricultural production.

Given the permanence of a substantial monetary disequilibrium, and the resulting inflationary pressures in the deregulated markets for agricultural products, high price levels prevail that facilitate very high levels of profit for sellers in these markets.[178] In so far as profit levels bear no relationship to the value of labour employed, so that they cannot be interpreted as social recognition of productive labour, it is the distortionary conditions in which the market has to operate, rather than the market itself which tend to produce perverse effects in the allocation of economic resources. The problem is especially acute in conditions, such as in Cuba, where both deregulated and extensive regulated markets function side by side, creating differences in prices and profitability

---

[176] We would like to point to an additional consequence for supply of the high concentration of liquidity in the form of deposits in the hands of a limited proportion of the population, although this is only a hypothesis and will require further in-depth study. The chain of value added of an important part of the private and state sectors depends on the development of agricultural production. However, the high levels of money held by some private peasant farmers, some cooperative sectors and their intermediaries has a paradoxical effect on production. In observations and interviews carried out by the authors with various peasant producers, some very relevant information came out. The high sums held as deposits do not correspond only to the propensity for 'atavistic' savings, but also to the inadequacy of means of channelling such funds to investment. When a given level of consumption is reached, 'positive' incentives to work are weakened. On the other hand, the security that individuals derive from the possession of large saving deposits practically makes 'negative' incentives disappear.

[177] Those which show greater sensitivity to the relationship between the quantity of demand and changes in prices. This is not the case in the farmers' market in Cuba, where demand is maintained at high levels in spite of high prices, since these are goods of the most basic necessity.

[178] In passing it is worth reiterating that high prices in such markets are not just the result of insufficient supply. This is an important factor, but it should not minimise the inflationary pressures that result from the acute monetary imbalance which already exists. To assume that de-regulated markets, even in conditions of greater supply, could function free from distortions in the presence of significant monetary imbalances is to fail to learn the lessons of the history of markets.

which spread the distortionary effects through the whole agricultural sector.[179] It is clear that while regulated and de-regulated markets exist within the same sector distortionary tendencies will remain, but the point we are making is that under conditions of acute monetary disequilibrium such distortions will become practically unmanageable through economic instruments.

The alternatives to de-monetisation

As indicated above, this section will present possible paths to a 'solution' to the still unresolved problem of passive liquidity, or in other terms, the problem of the concentration of accumulated liquidity.

In reality the conditions to confront the actual situation of excess liquidity are different and more complicated than those which existed in mid-1994, and have become more complicated,[180] requiring new reflections which are based on 'the real state of affairs'. Below we focus on various different options which are available now, making clear that we cannot cover all options or combinations of options but only those which we judge are more significant.

All the alternatives, however, need, as we have mentioned above, to be part of a coherent programme which reduces the risks of future de-stabilisation and which prioritises measures on the supply side to expand production and employment. On the other hand, it must be taken into account that, given the social and political dimensions, the specific form of demonetisation which will be adopted will depend on the general structure of the programme of transformation.

The principal alternatives which in our view are available are:

I. Continuation of a gradual demonetisation programme. We need to add to the analysis of the negative effects described above that within a dynamic perspective this alternative will lead to a *de facto* 'adversely selective'

---

[179]   In Cuba the problem is very worrying in that the most important agricultural export products (sugar cane, coffee, tobacco) only trade in regulated markets. The differences in profitability between a field planted with coffee rather than sweet potato, for example, could be stark. To prevent this resulting in an adverse allocation of resources requires extra-economic procedures, and even then the problem cannot be resolved. In Cuba, where access to land is not free, the production of crops for regulated markets should be the gateway to the production of economic activities which have highly profitable niches (for example, areas of *autoconsumo*). Under these conditions there is always the danger of the possible mis-allocation of resources in order to devote them to the more lucrative marginal production. There is even a popular term to describe this phenomenon: *conuquear* (*conuquero* = smallholder).

[180]   The opening of larger spaces in the market, the growing presence of the private, national cooperative and foreign investment sectors, the issuing of the convertible peso, and the subsequent establishment of exchange offices are factors that modify the situation which must be taken into account in future decisions about routes to demonetisation.

privatisation of the economic spaces being opened. This process, although it is relatively gradual, is nevertheless very problematic, as it is carried out in conditions of extreme inequality in the holding of money-capital, which excludes wide sectors of the population and conflicts with key values of society.

After a period of operation this alternative has revealed important structural faults such as its incapacity to act in the face of the concentration of monetary holdings and the premature exhaustion of the possibilities of gaining sustained access to money holdings for the majority of the population as the principal source of demonetisation.

It could be thought that the adoption of a skewed taxation policy directed at groups holding concentrations of liquidity – and those groups with higher incomes – will resolve these problems. However, there are various considerations here; first, the establishment of progressive taxes will be on the basis of incomes,[181] not on accumulated deposits, and this presents some problems. The new tax system proposed is not specifically related to bank accounts. These will only be affected to the extent that the measures will produce variations in savings to compensate for the income confiscated by the government in the form of taxes and withdrawn from monetary circulation. Even in this case the process would continue to be slow and would maintain the inflationary pressures and distortions described above over a time period which we consider unnecessarily long and which would make problematic the effectiveness of other economic measures.

We need to take into account that the recuperation of the value of the national currency in order to strengthen incentives to work is not a process which rests solely on the scarcity of money, in particular in the hands of the waged sectors. This process must more than anything have a positive impact on production because there exists a balance between the incomes of workers and the possibility of participating in a sustained manner in the markets. In conditions of acute distortion of real prices (both in the de-regulated and the foreign exchange markets), the effect of money shortages on work will have very precise limits and could generate other undesired effects.

The slowness of the process will continue to act as an important advantage for those sectors with concentrations of liquidity *vis-à-vis* the rest of the population. The fact that in the future the government could redistribute part of these incomes is, in most cases, only a small consolation which does not resolve the larger problem which in our view must be observed in a socialist programme: the necessity of minimising the social, political and ideological trauma that, in a society such as Cuba, the development of a permanent form of

---

[181]   There are other taxes specifically directed to these social sectors such as inheritance tax, property and property transfer taxes and others, but in general the most significant are progressive income taxes.

structural social differentiation represents.[182] This could become more problematic when one takes into account that in future the government could adopt measures aimed at establishing new types of non-state enterprises.[183]

II. 'Forced' and 'voluntary' savings. 'Forced' savings consists of non-confiscatory money exchange with compulsory deposit in bank accounts above a certain sum.[184] This would allow the withdrawal of liquidity in a way which is spread over time, prioritising certain objectives.[185] It would have the advantage of neutralising the inflationary potential of existing passive liquidity. Also, to the extent that this would in fact represent a relative revaluation of wages and pensions, it would have an immediate beneficial impact on equity. It would have the potential negative effect of the high internal debt taken on by the state.

Another form of organising 'forced' savings would be the conversion of sums of money above a certain limit into investment instruments, which could be utilised to buy assets in state enterprises being privatised, or for new investment. This would require complementary efforts in the articulation of a market for intermediate goods and capital. It is clear that this would be its most controversial political effect and it would maintain the initial differences, although dampened, in conditions of already relatively deregulated markets and the growing presence of the private sector.

'Voluntary' savings, *via* the purchase of state bonds, would not require a monetary exchange. But this may not have an appreciable effect on the reduction of liquidity in circulation unless the savings can be channelled into investment in the private and cooperative sector. This would also represent a high level of internal debt for the government.

This alternative, in whichever of its variants, would be a *de facto* 'economic amnesty', since it would legitimate the concentration in liquidity. It would also have political costs associated with the temporary illiquidity of funds, and, to the extent that it represents a quasi-confiscatory measure, would raise concerns about confiscatory actions.

III. Proportional currency replacement. This would consist of a monetary substitution, replacing current pesos with a new peso according to a fixed ratio

---

[182]   By way of illustration only, and to put the problem into perspective, in June 1995 the ordinary savings in the hands of 14% of savers was 50% higher than the level of planned investment in the national budget for the whole of that year.

[183]   This possibility was announced by the Minister of Economy and Planning during the second conference on 'The nation and emigration' held in Havana at the beginning of November 1995. See the journal *Trabajadores*, Havana, 6 November 1995.

[184]   The alternative to this is only a partial freezing of bank accounts without a monetary substitution, but in essence this is the same mechanism.

[185]   If one such objective were to be investment, this would be dealt with by policies that are explained immediately below.

– for example, five pesos equals one new peso. This would imply a relative re-valuation of wages and pensions, and thus would have a positive impact on equity. This would also reproduce, though in a mitigated way, the initial differentiations.

In addition to not substantially modifying the initial unequal distribution in liquidity, this has the further political cost of being a measure that will affect the whole population without discrimination, and although its future effects on income distribution should be progressive, in the short run it will definitely provoke a hostile response. On the other hand, it is expected that it will produce a sudden fall in aggregate demand, and probably in supply, from the non-state sector.[186] An alternative way to achieve similar results could be to apply a given multiplier to all prices and wages simultaneously. Psychologically the opposition might be less, but it would carry costs in terms of the correlation of data throughout the economy as well as the problems initially caused by the physical quantity of money required for transactions.

IV. Sale of high value consumer goods. The sale of articles of consumption of high value, such as houses, cars etc., would have a negative impact because of the high foreign exchange cost for the government as well as the associated political costs.[187] On the other hand, it is not always easy to differentiate between consumer goods and capital goods. Some variant of this measure could complement other policies that would act directly on the problem.

V. Direct sales of state assets. The direct sale of state assets[188] is the rapid route suggested by some of those who have faith in the restoration of a 'market economy' in Cuba. It would be based on an initial situation of relative inequality with all the social and political problems which have been discussed earlier.[189] In addition, we can assume that if it should be wished to channel the maximum possible amount of savings towards investment, it would probably be necessary

---

[186] The impact of this will be proportionate to the participation of the non-state sector in the economy.

[187] The problem of housing is a key matter in any debate. There are many *micro-brigadistas* who have been allocated to social works over a prolonged period, waiting for housing to be built or finished.

[188] This is different from the 'forced savings' mechanism described above in the sense that it concerns direct sales to those holding monetary assets without the obligation of participating in a programme of converting savings into an investment instrument.

[189] On this point it is important to emphasise that, different from most of the proposals for the establishment of a market economy in Cuba which separate 'privatisation' from macro-stabilisation, Andrew Zimbalist and Manuel Pastor have outlined a programme in which the privatisation of state assets would be an essential component for economic stabilisation. They introduce a series of measures which try to take into account social differentiation and the political problems associated with a transformation of this type. Apart from our fundamental disagreement with proposals of this nature, we acknowledge that the programme suggested, in addition to being technically rational, is based on a social sensitivity which is not common in literature on this theme. It deserves further discussion which, for reasons of space, is not possible within this book. See Pastor and Zimbalist (1995).

to introduce a market in land, given the provenance and interests of a major part of the concentration of cash holdings. This would imply a social debate of enormous magnitude and relevance that, in our view, is not a priority in the current debate about restructuring the Cuban economy.

We believe that the indiscriminate application of this measure is politically unsound, contrary to a socialist restructuring and, besides, will not in itself guarantee the disappearance of the inflationary potential residing in accumulations of liquidity, which could fall out of control in the new spaces of the market which are opening.

In our thinking, the opening of larger spaces for non-state forms of ownership (cooperative or private) is a necessary process, but one which must have clear extra-economic limits and effective economic regulations so that it does not drift into structures that are opposed to a socialist restructuring.

VI. A limited confiscatory currency replacement, linked to a proportionate progressive exchange. As we noted earlier, we favour a monetary substitution with partially progressive confiscation.[190] However, since between the preparation of the manuscript and the first edition of this book the premises for a monetary substitution based on confiscating part of accumulated savings above given levels had changed, we proposed, in a footnote, a less radical form of replacement. We considered then that the new conditions created by the opening of the farmers' markets, and other de-regulated markets made it advisable to exclude from the confiscatory substitutions deposits made after 1 October 1994. We also allowed that such deposits could be subject to 'forced savings' measures.

In our view 1 October 1994, the date of the most significant opening of the internal markets so far, is an important reference point in terms of any future economic policy since it is necessary to maintain the credibility of decisions taken by the government.[191]

At this point it is worth repeating two points: first, we still consider that it is necessary to take measures to de-monetise the economy in the short run, and secondly the opening of the farmers' markets and later developments in this area effectively modified the starting point for a confiscatory currency replacement.

The opening of greater spaces in the market and the extension of the private and cooperative sectors have legitimised accumulations during that period and introduced new considerations concerning the recessive effects of a currency

---

[190]   We consider that during the first 9 months of 1994 such a policy had a certain degree of social consensus.

[191]   The opening of market opportunities and the development of non-state economic activities should only have taken place once a functional level of internal financial equilibrium had been established.

replacement on these markets and sectors. On the other hand, external actors, with a growing presence as the result of the government's efforts and success in attracting foreign investment, might perceive a radical confiscatory monetary substitution as a sign of 'counter-reform'.

However, we consider that within the context of an integrated programme of transformation, a partial confiscatory substitution of the national currency is still the most appropriate way to achieve the functional de-monetisation of the economy needed to create better conditions to continue the process of change.

It would have a positive impact on the distribution of cash holdings and, in the long run, of income, since it will substantially reduce differences between individuals operating in the new market spaces and the expansion of the non-state sectors in the domestic economy. In the context of a still weak progressive taxation policy, and given the reduced redistributive capacity of the government, its effect on equity will be favourable, at least compared with the present situation.

Such a measure would neutralise to a sufficient extent the potential inflationary effect of money holdings; and, if it is carried out at the right moment, the levels of internal debt it would create would be manageable.

In the beginning, its recessive impact, particularly on the non-state sector would be problematic. However, after that stage it would allow a greater degree of freedom for economic policy to increase aggregate demand by using, above all, monetary policy. This, together with supply-side measures, would lead to an increase in production and employment in the cooperative and private sectors, which would have to act in a context of greater financial tension. This would be a stimulus to increasing the intensity and effectiveness of labour, by seeking new bases for profitability and accumulation, but now within legal conditions and under clear regulations guaranteed by the government. This will create better conditions to rationalise the labour force in the state sector and to promote the effective articulation of the non-state sector as well as policies to protect the more vulnerable social sectors.

An additional disadvantage would be the relatively greater political cost, compared to that of a currency exchange if it had been carried out in 1994, given that not all those active as private agents since October 1994 have deposited their money in the banking system.[192] A point to consider is the compensatory effect of the response, which would be at least neutral, of a large part of the population, whose incomes would be revalued following the monetary

---

[192]   Here we are thinking of a measure in which bank deposits made since 1 October 1994 would be exchanged without confiscation.

substitution.[193] Other disadvantages are similar to those accruing from the alternative plans for a confiscatory substitution originally proposed.[194]

To counter the degree of uncertainty such a measure would create both within the society and amongst external actors, it should be represented as part of an integrated programme of restructuring which would represent the social consensus, reinforce the credibility of economic policy, make use of recent structural economic transformations, and provide a clear direction for the future.

Our Proposal

Our preference is for alternative VI, that is, a programme of demonetisation based centrally, though not exclusively, on a currency substitution with limited confiscatory measures *via* a proportionately progressive currency exchange rate. This alternative is described below:

– all existing cash would be exchanged, both cash in savings accounts and that which remained in the hands of the population;[195]

– existing cash would be exchanged in progressive proportions, at intervals above a given limit;

– cash up to a certain previously determined limit would be exempt from confiscation (taking into account the sum of cash in circulation and ordinary savings);

– increases in cash balances after 1 October 1994 (date of the opening of the farmers' markets) would be exempt from confiscation, taking care not to damage the credibility of previous measures taken by the government;[196]

– cash exchanged (above a given level) would be compulsorily deposited in a bank account, and the withdrawal of only a limited amount in a given period would be authorised;

– a special system could be established for withdrawal from deposited surpluses for certain categories such as peasant farmers, cooperatives and others for whom cash is also productive capital, according to the priorities

[193] It should be remembered that the confiscation would only affect those who possessed deposits above a certain limit, that is a minority of the population, given the degree of current concentration of liquidity. In June 1995 more than 86% of savings account were less than 2,000 pesos.

[194] An additional complication to be considered is the level of issue of convertible pesos, and their growing introduction into circulation *via* the exchange houses.

[195] We would not exclude the possibility of introducing a more radical version with the requirement that anyone changing cash above a given limit would have to prove it was obtained legally. If they were not able to do so, all cash above the limit would be confiscated.

[196] Additional exceptions for other categories of deposits could be established.

of economic policy;

– bank deposits would not be indexed.[197]

Below we illustrate this proposal with a hypothetical example. For an individual who possessed 4,000 pesos in cash and 57,000 pesos in bank deposits (of which 30,000 pesos had been deposited since 1 October 1994) the process of substitution would be as follows:

Table 3

Level of Cash Holdings	Substitution ratio	Pre-currency exchange	Post-currency exchange
First 2,000 (cash held before 1 Oct. 1994: 31,000)	1 x 1	2,000	2,000
From 2,000 to 20,000	1 x 0.33	18,000	5,940
More than 20,000	1 x 0.10	11,000	1,100
Increase in bank balance after 1 Oct. 1994: 30,000	1 x 1	30,000	30,000
Total		61,000	39,040

Note: The intervals and ratios of monetary substitutions used in this example are solely to facilitate comparison and do not represent a concrete proposal for such a measure; these must be established on the basis of rigorous analysis of available data.

Finally we repeat our criterion that the measures described above must be conceived as part of an integrated and explicit programme of economic restructuring which, in a continuous form, will modify the causes of financial disequilibrium; this is a key element.[198] In the context of such a programme, the measures taken will not have the same significance or effectiveness if viewed separately as they will if viewed as a whole as an economic programme.

Currency replacement is a central measure for the demonetisation of the economy, a necessary condition to ensure that the whole process of adjustment and later reforms is viable, not just from the economic perspective but also from the political and social points of view.

This central measure should be accompanied by other complementary

---

[197] The non-indexation of bank deposits represents an additional instrument of demonetisation, since any future price increases would reduce the value of cash held in deposits.

[198] As we have already emphasised in Chapters 3 and 4.

measures such as the sale of certain luxury goods. The other measures which have formed part of this gradual demonetisation option (prices, taxes, tariffs etc.) will, from this perspective, have the function of maintaining and regulating the equilibria previously accomplished.

In particular, the implementation of monetary substitution in the initial phase would favour the creation of conditions needed to raise the effectiveness of the state sector and is an indispensable premise for the construction of a market which is not based on a perverse distribution of money. One of the points of departure for the present changes in Cuba, which has not been resolved as the result of the measures adopted so far, has been the unequal distribution of money. This largely benefits people who have accumulated wealth from illegal activities or on the basis of unearned profits obtained as the result of the economic situation prevailing in the country over the last few years. This is a situation which must be changed; if not, income will continue to be concentrated and this sector will be placed in an advantageous position in regard to new market opportunities as they are created.

Demonetisation through currency replacement would also allow functional equilibria to be re-established that would take into account the disequilibrium levels of prices, and would reduce the distortionary conditions which prevail in some important markets in Cuba. It would give a true sense to the connection between work and income and will make it possible to dismantle the regressive measures that adversely affect the majority of the population.

We consider that any decision about demonetisation should be made as the result of a wide social debate, given its political implications. Our objective has been to encourage reflection on an issue that we consider relevant to the future of the country.

Conclusions

These reflections on restructuring will not answer all the questions that are current or foreseeable and we have probably left out some that require attention. In particular, we have not dealt with the complex and important questions of the level of popular participation required to proceed to the new model at which our proposals are directed. Also, the proposals set out in this book are controversial and therefore, no doubt, not without errors.

The basic proposal which has stimulated this effort was not to elaborate a programme of economic restructuring which is totally finished and infallible, an *ex ante* design of all necessary actions to be taken. This level of perfection in the field of economic prescription, although desirable, is not achievable. Beyond the human limitations which are surely present in this work, the configuration of medium and long-term economic plans will depend to a great degree on the evolution of the context in which such plans are designed to act, and for this reason the definitive measures to be taken have to be varied according to the rich variety that reality always presents.

Even more important is that our proposal does not assume that an harmonic equilibrium is a 'natural state of affairs' in the new socialist model which we are trying to achieve, and much less do we consider that the economic restructuring project that we consider necessary for this will be balanced and free from conflicts.

However, we think we have elaborated an economic restructuring programme with a socialist economic orientation to take into account the reality of the country. In terms of the 'architecture' of the programme, the emphasis has been placed on its integrated nature and the coherence of its components. All consideration of effectiveness and convenience of individual measures has been subordinated to achieve this systematic end.

To a great extent our thinking has been directed to an attempt to resolve a problem that should not be disregarded: the current challenge for the Cuban economy is not only or exclusively the recovery of economic growth, but also to ensure that the basis of this growth contains an economic and social structure corresponding to the socialist paradigm that we aim to construct. The necessity to have a conceptual paradigm serving as an organisational centre for the work has required the adoption of an unconventional perspective on socialism, or to be precise, on its past, present and future. The construction of a regulated market in means of production within a socialist economy is the principal element of the programme and this defines it as a fundamental economic reform. On this is based the reconstruction of a viable socialist economy in Cuba, even though this viability is marred by extra-economic factors such as the hostile policies of the US government.

The programme proposed here is clearly polemical and the controversy is welcome when it serves to improve the objective of the activity – in this case the welfare of the Cuban people. The reactivation of the Cuban economy is a theme which interests many people and which arouses passions – at times quite unsuspected in many people – and this is understandable because behind the cold figures and the analysis of the economic variables hides the enormous effort the Cuban people have had to make since 1990 in order to survive the severe economic crisis exacerbated by the blockade. What happens now in economic matters will determine in large measure the fate of future generations of Cubans.

The economic restructuring proposed here undoubtedly contains an element of passion, probably matched by those who will question it. However, we have tried to present the material in a form that will contribute to the debate in the most rational way possible – above all, because serious discussion is the most important immediate 'way-stage' towards which this work is aimed.

Studies on reform in other countries and possible lessons for Cuba

Juan J. Buttari, 'Reflections on Systemic Economic Policy Reform: Lessons, Evaluations and Social Costs', in George P. Montalván (ed.), *Cuba in Transition. Volume 2: Papers and Proceedings of the Second Annual Meeting of the Association for the Study of the Cuban Economy*, Miami, Florida International University, 1993.

Jan Svejnar and Jorge Pérez-López, 'A Strategy for the Economic Transformation of Cuba based on the East European Experience', in Carmelo Mesa Lago (ed.), *Cuba After the Cold War*, Pittsburgh, University of Pittsburgh Press, 1993.

Jorge Pérez-López, 'Economic Reform in Cuba: Lessons from Eastern Europe', mimeo, April 1991.

– 'Learning from Others: Economic Reform Experiences in Eastern Europe, Latin America and China', in *Cuba in Transition. Study prepared by Florida International University (FIU) for US Department of State*, 1993.

Ernesto Hernández-Catá, 'Long Term Objectives and Transitional Policies. A Reflection on Pazos' "Economic Problems of Cuba"', in George P. Montalván (ed.), *Cuba in Transition. Volume 1: Papers and Proceedings of the Second Annual Meeting of the Association for the Study of the Cuban Economy*, Miami, Florida International University, 1992.

Proposals for reform explicitly related to Cuba

Jorge Sanguinetty (1992), 'El Desarrollo de una Economía de Mercado: el Caso de Cuba', in George P. Montalván (ed.), *Cuba in Transition. Volume 1: Papers and Proceedings of the Second Annual Meeting of the Association for the Study of the Cuban Economy*, Miami, Florida International University.

– (1993) 'The Transition Towards a Market Economy in Cuba: Its Legal and Managerial Dimensions', *Cuba in Transition. Study prepared by Florida International University (FIU) for US Department of State.*

Felipe Pazos (1992), 'Problemas Económicos de Cuba en el Período de Transición', in George P. Montalván (ed.), *Cuba in Transition. Volume 1: Papers and Proceedings of the Second Annual Meeting of the Association for the Study of the Cuban Economy*, Miami, Florida International University.

Rolando H. Castañeda (1992), 'Cuba: Una Opción por la Libertad, el Desarrollo y la Paz Social (Propuesta de Lineamientos Estratégicos para la Completa Transformación de la Economía Socialista a una Economía Social de Mercado)', in George P. Montalván (ed.), *Cuba in Transition. Volume 1: Papers and Proceedings of the Second Annual Meeting of the Association for the Study of the Cuban Economy*, Miami, Florida International University.

– (1993a) 'Cuba: Fundamentos de una propuesta para el establecimiento y desarrollo de una economía social de mercado', in George P. Montalván (ed.), *Cuba in Transition. Volume 2: Papers and Proceedings of the Second Annual Meeting of the Association for the Study of the Cuban Economy*, Miami, Florida International University.

– (1993b) 'Cuba: Central Elements of a Stabilization Program and the Initiation of Economy-Wide Structural Reforms', *Cuba in Transition. Study prepared by Florida International University (FIU) for US Department of State.*

Rolando H. Castañeda and George P. Montalván (1993), 'In Search of a Way Out for Cuba: Reconciliation, Stabilization and Structural Reform', mimeo. Paper prepared for the annual meeting of the Eastern Economic Association, Washington D.C, March.

Sergio Roca (1993), 'Cuban Privatization: Potential Path and Implementation', *Cuba in Transition. Study prepared by Florida International University (FIU) for US Department of State.*

Carmelo Mesa-Lago (1993), 'The Social Safety Net in the Two Cuban Transitions', *Cuba in Transition. Study prepared by Florida International University (FIU) for US Department of State.*

Manuel Pastor and Andrew Zimbalist (1995), 'Waiting for Change: Adjustment and Reform in Cuba', *World Development*, Vol. 23, No. 5.

Business improvement schemes in military enterprises

In 1987, in the face of the problems in the System of State Planning of the Economy, which had been in operation since the 1970s, the Council of Ministers authorised the launch of an experiment in military enterprises (whose employees are, in large part, civilians) aiming to find a more efficient system of business management. This is referred to as 'Business Management Improvement'.

Its main components were: the introduction of modern management techniques (particularly participatory techniques), company restructuring placing emphasis on the specialisation and autonomy of basic units, the organisation of productive processes, flexibilisation of labour and wage policy, the introduction of new, modern systems of costing, greater flexibility in the elements of planning – reducing those which are directive in character and emphasising the role of financial indicators – and quality guarantee procedures, including quality circles.

In other sectors of the Cuban economy also, new techniques have been tried in business management. The Ministry of Basic Industry initiated, at the beginning of the 1980s, a process of improvement in efficiency of production. In spite of the good results registered in various aspects, the lack of integration and the excessive regulation of prices, wages, supplies etc. prevented better results from being achieved. In contrast with the 'Business Management Improvement' scheme, the Ministry of Basic Industry was not given scope wide enough to enable it act independently of the majority of the established national regulations.

The Role of Planning in the Business Improvement Schemes in Military Enterprises

One of the most important changes introduced by the Business Improvement schemes was the reduction in the number of planning indicators to just four, which was much fewer than previously. These were:

- Selection of products
- Sales
- Net productivity
- Surplus

However, the level of autonomy in the management of indicators that are considered to be in force was more important than the reduction in the number of those indicators. Two principal aspects should be emphasised:

    – The indicator 'Selection of Products' includes only part of the total output. As the remaining part of the output is planned in a decentralised manner, room is created for a significant degree of inter-company coordination.

– Indicators such as 'Salaries Fund' (Fondo de Salarios) and 'Average Number of Workers' (Promedio de Trabajadores) are not considered to be directives. The inclusion of 'Net Productivity'[199] as a directive allows for a greater degree of autonomy in the management of the salaries fund and the number of workers, a traditional complaint among state enterprise managers in Cuba ever since the System of Direct Control and Planning in the Economy was implemented in the mid-1970s.

However, it should be noted that the salaries fund should be controlled selectively and with discretion, since price distortions, changes in types of product and involvement in one-off, not repeated productions can conceal wage increases that are not due to real increases in productivity.

In addition to the directive indicators, the plan also includes other, normative, indicators and limits which are not obligatory, although failure to meet them may imply economic sanctions.

Aspects of Labour and Wage Policy in the Business Improvement Scheme of Military Enterprises

The flexibility granted to military enterprises 'in the course of improvement' has resulted in an increase in productivity and a reduction in the labour force. The basic features of the experiment in the areas of labour and wages are:

– The 'ideal' nature of the qualifications required to occupy posts in the work force, which has implied a high level of demand in respect to the specific qualities needed by a worker to take up a particular post.

– Systems of payment: the re-institution of the principle of payment according to results has resulted in many ways of linking wages with productive efficiency, from well-known systems such as payment by piece-work to systems based on profit sharing.

– Flexibility in the definition of tasks and extension of the wage range. There is not a standard national set of job descriptions; each entity determines its own specific posts, according to the conditions of its productive process. In addition, the maximum wage on the scale has increased, allowing for greater wage differentiation between simple tasks and those that are more complex.

---

[199] Net productivity is the relation between net output and the average number of workers.

Sources:

MINFAR (1989), *Bases generales del Perfeccionamiento en el MINFAR*, Grupo de Perfeccionamiento de las Organizaciones Empresariales e Instituciones del MINFAR.

Lázaro Lamar, Armando Pérez, and Berto González (1989), 'El perfeccionamiento de los sistemas de costos en el MINFAR', *Cuba Socialista*, No. 40, July-Aug.

Armando Pérez and Berto González (1988), 'El perfeccionamiento empresarial en el MINFAR', *Cuba Socialista*, No. 36, Nov.-Dec.

– (1990), 'La organización de la producción en el perfeccionamiento empresarial de las FAR', *Cuba Socialista*, No. 44, April-June.

ANNEX 4

Repressed inflation

This is the second time in the Revolutionary era that the problem of excess money in circulation has assumed critical proportions.[200] However, on the first occasion.in the 1970s there was the genuine possibility of a rapid reactivation of supply through an increase in the national production of consumer goods and through imports, essentially from the old socialist countries.

The present situation is different. Rapid recovery in supply does not seem likely, at least in the short term. The policy of bringing about adjustment without inflation, which was necessary from the political and social point of view, has become an immediate cause of excess circulation.

The maintenance of fixed consumer prices, regardless of the significant drop in supply, generates a repressed inflation in the state market for consumer goods, which is then released into the non-state market, in which own-account workers, speculators and peasant farmers are active as the main sellers. A large part of the goods and services transacted are illegal in origin. Any transaction carried out in this non-state market is highly profitable.[201]

We will attempt below to examine more deeply three aspects related to the high profitability attained by sellers in the non-state market, and the resulting concentration of cash. It is worth pointing out that concentration of income is a characteristic of any free market, but what we are concerned with here is to identify these characteristics in the Cuban reality and also the factors that encourage it.

---

[200]   At the end of the 1960s an excess of money in circulation was experienced, caused mainly by the policy of state transfers and the abandonment of the linkage between wages and productive output. For an analysis of this, see 'Informe del Comité Central del PCC al Congreso', *El Militante Comunista* (Jan-Feb. 1976), pp. 63-4.

[201]   The high profitability of the informal sector creates tensions between it and the state sector in the allocation of labour. In mid-1994 the authors conducted interviews with own-account workers in the sectors of food processing, shoemaking and shoe repairs, and gas lighter fillers. The individual with the lowest reported net income (discounting taxes and the cost of raw materials) had an average *daily* income of between 150 and 200 pesos, practically the average *monthly* salary of a state sector worker. This hyper-distortion contrasts with what has been observed in Latin America generally. In a study carried out in eight countries (Argentina, Brazil, Panama, Guatemala, Uruguay, Venezuela, Paraguay, and Mexico), in three of them the incomes of salaried workers were higher than those of own-account workers, in another four countries the incomes of workers in the informal sector were slightly higher than that of salaried workers, and in only one case were the incomes of informal sector workers twice those of the formal sector. See Rosenbluth (1994).

Fixing consumer prices below free market prices

The fixing of the prices of basic consumer goods at levels that enable their purchase by all citizens has been a policy of the Revolution. This has been sustained by means of a policy of subsidies on those goods. Logically, in the market for those goods – which, in addition, were rationed – a relative scarcity was experienced in relation to effective total demand. The parallel market resolved the problem, and avoided the uncontrolled growth in excess circulation.

From 1990, when the crisis made it impossible to sustain the parallel market, its place in meeting the demand that was not satisfied in the rationed market was taken over by the non-state market referred to at the start of this Annex. The subsidies contained in prices that are fixed by the state are transferred *via* the non-state market to private sellers. The population then becomes only the intermediary for the subsidy. Although the aim of the present analysis is to examine the current situation of the country, certain more general conclusions can be drawn.

Profitability of the non-state market before the 1990s

While the profitability available to sellers in this market has increased significantly in the present situation, it is also true that a high profit rate in the non-state market has been quite evident at other times, and in some specific activities, such as the free peasant farmers' market, it has never been totally absent.[202]

The economic rents that farmers and intermediaries obtained in this market were caused by the deficient supply structure in the state and cooperative sectors, and by the fixing of prices in the state market at levels below equilibrium. Thus, an important cause of the high incomes obtained by peasant farmers was the distortion in the market from agrarian goods. One part of the non-state market represents what in other countries is called the informal market. But in general terms the situation with regard to their profitability is completely different to what is found in Cuba.

---

[202] The free farmers' markets began in 1980, allowing individual peasant farmers and cooperatives to offer their excess production at market prices, after completing their obligatory quota of sales to the government. State enterprises could also engage in this market with the excess from their self-consumption plots. As well as being an extremely imperfect market, it fostered a number of distortions, such as sale of goods that had been stolen from state entities, and failure to comply with the obligatory supply to the state. In 1986 it was decided to close these markets, arguing, among other things, that they hindered cooperativisation.

Barriers to entry into the non-state market

The approval of Decree Law 141 and Joint Resolution No. 1 CETSS-CEF opened legal spaces in the non-state market. The concentration of income that is created in any market process, reinforced by repressed inflation in the state market for consumer goods, is further stimulated by the barriers to entry in this market. We have analysed these barriers as four: psychological, legal, material and informational.

Psychological. For a long time, extending up to the present moment, own-account work has been seen as socially negative. In addition, a large part of the raw materials used in own-account work is illegal in source, and many citizens avoid transactions that, if not precisely illegal, have hints of illegality.

Legal. Joint Resolution No. 1 fixed limits on who was entitled to carry out own-account work, and the requirements for this.[203]

Material. These barriers arise from the fact that there is no general market for materials and tools (means of production) for the sellers. Some of these goods are available in outlets that carry out their sales transactions in foreign currency, to which a minimum number of citizens have access.

Informational. The great fragmentation of the markets, and the lack of information and publicity, limit entry by potential sellers because of the uncertainty concerning engagement in certain economic activities.

These barriers, which reduce the number of sellers, and the lack of communications and transport that are created *sui generis* by monopolies and oligopolies, combine to make this a highly lucrative market.

Other distortions

A significant part of the materials and tools used in the production of goods, together with other goods themselves, are taken from the state sector without cost to the producers or to the sellers. Sellers also benefit from goods acquired in the state network at prices lower than equilibrium, which make extraordinary profits possible. In other words, products are acquired in the state sector at subsidised prices, but the goods produced with them are sold at market prices.

In the face of these three elements – fixing of prices below equilibrium, entry barriers, and other distortions referred to above – corrective action by the state is needed to improve the operation of the non-state market. If this primitive

---

[203]   The existence of legal barriers, together with the suspension of the issue of new permits for own-account work in certain activities, meant that non-authorised producers sold their produce to those who had licenses; the latter thus became legal traders for illegal producers.

market is to be the starting point for the construction of a socialist market involving state, cooperative and private entities, it must from the beginning be corrected through actions that avoid not only the 'failures' of the market, but also the 'failures' of the government that can create damaging distortions in the functioning of the market.

ANNEX 5

Monetary circulation and the rate of exchange

Unification of monetary circulation

Unification of the markets that are at present fragmented by monetary dualism – affecting the supply of goods and services to the people, to foreign tourists, to the state sector, cooperatives and the private sector – is essential in order to provide incentives to labour and to facilitate relations between the different economic agents. This unification will be achieved only gradually. Initially its central components will be the reinforcement, to the maximum that this is possible, of the use of national currency in individual commercial transactions and the establishment of a single exchange rate[204] for the Cuban peso. At later stages in the restructuring process the restrictions on use of foreign currency will be extended to other spheres. The process of monetary unification as a whole would include various types of exchange controls.

In the first phase of the programme, monetary unification would mean that all foreigners, Cuban citizens and the private and cooperative sectors would have to use the national currency to access the retail market in goods and services, whether state or mixed, which previously operated in foreign currency.

The gradual unification of the markets will be closely connected with a series of measures that would have been adopted earlier, and with other actions that would form part of the later stages in the restructuring programme. In particular, the programme would require an especially close relationship between exchange, monetary and fiscal policies in order to progress towards the establishment and stabilisation of a unified market.

The change of money, together with increases in prices of basic goods and the fixing of prices for other goods on a supply-and-demand basis, create the conditions, from the initial phase of the programme, for a plan to do away with currency dualism. It should be remembered that the economic adjustment carried out in the first phase will have produced a substantial demonetisation of the economy, and this will have favourable effects on the rate of exchange.

The restriction of the use of foreign currency in economic transactions (with the exceptions that will be necessary at each stage) will, from the beginning, establish the need for tourists, and Cuban citizens who receive remittances from abroad or other income in foreign currency, to exchange their foreign money for Cuban currency.

---

[204] The establishment of a single exchange rate does not exclude, however, the possibility of setting one or more exceptional rates for specific purposes.

The need for an economically based single exchange rate

In order to set a single exchange rate that will accurately reflect the expenditure in labour in Cuba in order to obtain a unit of foreign exchange, it is necessary to have a system of internal prices as free of distortions as possible.

In the case of Cuba, wholesale prices are significantly different from retail prices.[205] This has been a consequence of various factors, including a system of price rigidity based on costings that were planned but inaccurately determined, in large part due to inexact records of historic costs, and an insufficient profit margin applied to projected costs, failing to take into account periodic changes in real conditions. This generates insufficient levels of profit in the productive enterprise sector and, hence, imbalances in the budget that must then be financed through indirect taxes.

The calculation of an economically based rate of exchange[206] will be part of a profound change in internal prices, to reflect real conditions of production. This is a task that requires time, and in the first phase of the programme an interim measure would be applied, fixing an exchange rate specifically for tourists and Cuban citizens who receive income and remittances in foreign currency.

The exchange rate and the financing of consumer imports

As we have pointed out elsewhere in this book, one of the needs of the Cuban economy is to devote a determined quantity of foreign exchange to the production or importation of consumer goods in order to increase the intensity and productivity of labour. However, the scarcity of foreign currency imposes tight limits on the availability of these imports that, at present, are almost exclusively traded in foreign currency. In the context of the proposed programme, access in national currency to these imports, by all individuals and by the cooperative and private sectors, increases the population of possible buyers, and this gives special importance to the problem of financing of such imports. A viable solution would be for part of these imports to be financed essentially through tourist spending and the foreign currency income received by some Cuban citizens.[207]

---

[205] This was also a characteristic of the member countries of the former COMECON. This disparity makes it necessary to maintain a dual system of exchange rates. See Unanue and Rúa (1987).

[206] The determination of an economically based exchange rate could be achieved in other ways, requiring more detailed examination than is possible in a general proposal such as is made in this book. The choice of one method or another will depend on thorough, comprehensive work that Cuban specialists will have to carry out.

[207] This is only one of the variants. It could be decided to devote a determined quantity of foreign currency for import of consumer goods or for goods required in order to reactivate national production, in preference over other objectives.

The adoption of a *specific* rate for these purposes necessitates a detailed analysis. Two of the measures taken in the first phase create the necessary conditions for the adoption of such a rate:

- Reform of retail prices, with a reduction in the subsidies on products of basic necessity and an increase in other prices according to relationships of supply and demand, will reduce the excess money supply. This will be directed towards products that were previously available only for foreign currency.

- The change of national currency constitutes a rapid contraction in demand, with few additional recessive effects, on account of the pre-eminence of the state sector which, during the first phase, will not operate according to market principles. The type of currency change proposed here also reduces the concentration of income, contributing to the elimination, in large part, of a substantial demand that could arise in the sectors where cash is presently concentrated, for products that today are offered only for foreign currency and that from the first phase will be available for national currency.

Specific exchange rate for tourists and those with foreign currency income

The *specific* exchange rate proposed should guarantee that there are no increases in relative prices for consumer goods and services such as to discourage tourism or remittances from abroad. 'Anchored' dollar prices for products that are demanded essentially by tourists should not be affected.[208] On the other hand, a basis of calculation will be that higher dollar prices will be imposed for those products that do not affect tourist demand. Below we will illustrate with an example demonstrating the mechanism proposed for the initial calculation of the specific rate.

Initial example
The situation (greatly simplified) shown in the following table reflects hypothetically how the dollar sale of goods and services functions at present. (The example assumes the sale of just one product.)

---

[208] That is, goods and services that are offered to international tourists in national currency after the fixing of prices in that currency, and that are at present sold in foreign currency. It should be remembered that a considerable part of tourist expenditure (for example, air travel and tourist packages) is effected at the point of sale in other countries.

Groups	Demand in foreign currency ($US)	Price in dollars	Quantity bought
Tourists and individuals possessing foreign exchange	1,500	10	150
Rest of the population (without foreign exchange)	–	–	–
Total	1,500	N/A	150

The conditions assumed are as follows:

– the increase in relative price of the product (p) is 25 %[209]

– the population that does not have access to foreign currency will exercise an effective demand of 5,000 pesos in this market (Dm)

– price is set to clear the market with effective demand equal to the quantity offered

– the increase in the relative price of goods demanded by the population in foreign currency would finance completely the supply offered to the rest of the population

– the effective demand of tourists and Cuban citizens with foreign currency (Dd) will not change even though the price has increased and is assumed to be $1,500.

According to this example, the initial specific exchange rate (er) will be calculated as follows:

$$er = \left(\frac{Dm}{Dd*p}\right)*100 = \left(\frac{5,000}{1,500*25}\right)*100 = 13.33$$

To obtain access to the goods in this market both tourists and Cuban citizens with foreign currency will have to carry out the exchange into Cuban currency at the rate previously established.

The price of the article in Cuban currency will be as follows:

Price = $ 10.00 USD x 1.25 x 13.33 pesos/USD = 166.62 pesos

---

[209] Remember that only the relative price of products that do *not* affect tourist demand will be increased.

The result of this exercise is as follows:

Groups	Demand in Foreign Currency (US$)	Demand in Domestic Currency (pesos)	Price in pesos	Quantity sold
Tourists or individuals possessing foreign exchange	1500	19995	166.62	120
Rest of the population (without foreign exchange)	-	5000	166.62	30
Total	1500	24995	n.a.	150

Since the dimensions of this exchange rate depend on the demand of sectors that possess foreign currency and on the deliberate increase in prices, it should be recalculated periodically.

This example is extremely simple in its suppositions, but it gives an idea of how, in a demonetised economy, with a reasonable level of increase in relative prices, the parallel market can be reactivated in national currency supported partially or wholly by the increase in relative prices.

The relationship between monetary, fiscal and exchange rate policy

The system of social accounts and the different ways in which the Gross Domestic Product (GDP) can be expressed enables us to comprehend the enormous significance of coordinating policies. The following identities apply:

$X-M = (S-I) + (T-G)^{210}$, where:

X   : exports
M   : imports
S   : savings – private, cooperative and by decentralised state enterprises (after payment of direct taxes)
I   : investment – private, cooperative and by decentralised state enterprises
T   : budget income
G   : budget expenditure
S-I : savings gap
T-G : fiscal gap
X-M : external trade gap

Beginning with this stage, the size of S and I will increase with the decentralisation of state enterprises, so that credit policy will have to play a fundamental role in the maintenance of the level of imports according to the availability of foreign currency. Fiscal policy also acts directly on the size of the external trade gap and on the possibility of maintaining the rate of exchange.

Without diminishing the importance of management of aggregate demand by means of monetary and fiscal policy in order to influence the reduction of the external trade gap or the balance of trade, the demand for certain means of production and consumption may be inelastic and may affect the availability of foreign currency, creating bottle-necks. In this sense, it is indispensable, together with monetary and fiscal policies designed for external balance, to have an industrial policy that encourages export sectors and import substitution sectors, to adopt temporary trade barriers, and to effect control of the exchange rate.

Clearly, the size of the external trade gap does not only depend on the fiscal and savings gaps. The influx of external capital could allow the level of imports to be increased, but this would always have to be coordinated once again with monetary and fiscal policies.

---

[210] This identity is derived from the fact that GDP can be expressed (a) as the sum of expenditures and (b) as the sum of consumption and savings.

BIBLIOGRAPHY

Adam, Christopher, Cavendish, William and Mistry, Percy S. (1992), *Adjusting Privatization*, Villiers Publications, London.

Albert, Michel and Hahnel, Robin (1981), *Socialism Today and Tomorrow*, South End Press, Boston.

– (1983), 'Participatory planning', in Steve Rosskamm Shalom (ed.), *Socialist Visions*, South End Press, Boston.

– (1990a), *Quiet Revolution in Welfare Economics*, Princeton University Press, Princeton, NJ.

– (1990b), *Participatory Economics*, Princeton University Press, Princeton, NJ.

– (1990c), 'Cuba Si?', *Z Magazine*.

Alonso, Aurelio (1992), 'La economía cubana: los desafíos de un ajuste sin desocialización', *Cuadernos de Nuestra América*, Vol. IX, No. 19.

Alvarez Dozáguez, Armando (1993), 'Caña de azúcar: la materia prima más deficitaria hoy en la Patria de Alvaro Reinoso', (mimeo), La Habana, Dec.

Arenas, Patricia (1994), 'Para un enfoque psicosocial de la participación en Cuba', (mimeo), Fondo CIPS, La Habana.

Azcuy, Hugo (1992), 'Aspectos de la ley de reforma constitucional cubana de julio de 1992', (mimeo), Sección de Información Científica del Centro de Estudios sobre América (CEA), La Habana, July.

Banco Nacional de Cuba, *Informe Económico*, La Habana, Aug. 1995.

Bartell, Ernest (1993), 'Privatization: The Role of Domestic Business', Working Paper No. 198, Kellogg Institute, University of Notre Dame, South Bend.

Brus, Wlodzimierz (1972), *El funcionamiento de la economía socialista*, Editorial Oikos-Tau. S.A., España.

– (1985), 'Socialism – Feasible and Viable?, *New Left Review*, No. 153, Sept.-Oct.

Buttari, Juan J. (1993), 'Reflections on Systemic Economic Policy Reform: Lessons, Evaluations and Social Costs', in George P. Montalván (ed.), in *Cuba in Transition. Volume 2: Papers and Proceedings of the Second Annual Meeting of the Association for the Study of the Cuban Economy*, Miami, Florida International University.

Carranza Valdés, Julio (1992), 'Cuba: Los retos de la economía', *Cuadernos de Nuestra América*, Centro de Estudios sobre América, La Habana, Vol. IX, No. 19, July-Dec.

– (1994), 'Los cambios económicos en Cuba: problemas y desafíos', *Cuadernos de Nuestra América*, Centro de Estudios sobre América, La Habana Vol. XII, No. 22, July-Dec.

Castañeda, Rolando H. (1992), 'Cuba: Una Opción por la Libertad, el Desarrollo y la Paz Social (Propuesta de Lineamientos Estratégicos para la Completa Transformación de la Economía Socialista a una Economía Social de Mercado)', in George P. Montalván (ed.), in *Cuba in Transition. Volume 1: Papers and Proceedings of the Second Annual Meeting of the Association for the Study of the Cuban Economy*, Miami, Florida International University.

– (1993a), 'Cuba: Fundamentos de una propuesta para el establecimiento y desarrollo de una economía social de mercado', in George P. Montalván (ed.), in *Cuba in Transition. Volume 2: Papers and Proceedings of the Second Annual Meeting of the Association for the Study of the Cuban Economy*, Miami, Florida International University.

– (1993b), 'Cuba: Central Elements of a Stabilization Program and the Initiation of Economy-Wide Structural Reforms', in *Cuba in Transition. Study prepared by Florida International University for US Department of State*.

Castañeda, Rolando H. and Montalván, George P. (1993a), 'In Search of a Way Out for Cuba: Reconciliation, Stabilization and Structural Reform', mimeo. Paper prepared for the Annual Meeting of the Eastern Economic Association, Washington D.C, March.

– (1993b), 'Transition in Cuba: A comprehensive Stabilisation Proposal and some Key Issues', *Cuba in Transition*, Vol. 3, Florida International University, Miami.

CEPAL (1992), *Equidad y transformación productiva: un enfoque integrado*, Santiago de Chile.

Chen, Kang, Jefferson, Gary H., and Singh, Inderjit (1992), 'Lessons from China's Economic Reform', *Journal of Comparative Economics*, Vol. 16, No. 2 (June).

CONAS (1996), *Cuba: inversiones y negocios 1995-1996*, La Habana.

Davis, Jeffrey M. (ed.) (1992), *Macroeconomic Adjustment Policy. Instruments and Issues*, IMF Institute.

Devine, Pat (1988), 'Market Mania of the Left', *Marxism Today*, June.

Devlin, Robert (1993), 'Las privatizaciones y el bienestar social', *Revista de la CEPAL*, No. 49, Santiago de Chile.

Dilla, Haroldo (1992), 'Socialismo, empresas y participación obrera: notas para un debate cubano' (mimeo), La Habana.

– (1993), 'Cuba: la crisis y la rearticulación del consenso político (notas para un debate socialista), *Cuadernos de Nuestra América*, CEA, La Habana, Vol. X, No. 20, July-Dec.

Erber, Ernest (1990), 'Virtues and Vices of the Market', *Dissent*, Summer.

Feinerman, James V. (1991), 'Economic and Legal Reform in China', *Problems of Communism*, Sept.-Oct.

Fischer, Stanley (1993), *Does Macroeconomic Policy Matter?* Occasional Papers No. 27, International Center for Economic Growth, San Francisco.

Fischer, Stanley and Gelb, Alan (1990), 'Issues in Socialist Economic Reform', mimeo, Nov.

– (1991), 'The Process of Socialist Transformation', *Journal of Economic Perspectives*, Vol. 5, No. 4 (Fall).

González, Alfredo (1993), *Modelos económicos socialistas: escenarios para Cuba en los años noventa*. Instituto Nacional de Investigaciones Económicas, La Habana, May.

González, Gerardo (1992), 'Cuba y el mercado mundial: notas para una reflexión', *Revista Interamericana*, Vol. XXII, Nos. 3-4, Fall-Winter, San Juan, Puerto Rico.

Gutiérrez, Luis (1994), 'El estado como empresario en América Latina: ¿quo vadis?', *Cuadernos de Nuestra América*, Vol. XI, No. 22, Centro de

Estudios sobre América, La Habana, July-Dec.
- (1995), 'La eficiencia pública versus la privada. El mito y la evidencia', *Cuadernos de Nuestra América*, Vol. XII, No. 24, Centro de Estudios sobre América, La Habana, July-Dec.
Haimann, Theo and Scott, William G. (1977), *Dirección y gerencia*, Editorial Hispano Europea.
Hangren, Charles T. (1976), *Cost Accounting and Enterprise Management*, Ediciones Revolutionarias, Havana.
Harrold, Peter (1992), *China's Reform Experience to Date*, Discussion Paper No. 180, World Bank, Washington.
Hernández-Catá, Ernesto (1992), 'Long Term Objectives and Transitional Policies. A Reflection on Pazos' "Economic Problems of Cuba"', in George P. Montalván (ed.), in *Cuba in Transition. Volume 1: Papers and Proceedings of the Second Annual Meeting of the Association for the Study of the Cuban Economy*, Miami, Florida International University.
Jones, Susan K. (1991), 'El camino de la privatización', in *Finanzas y Desarrollo*, Banco Mundial, Washington D.C.
Kornai, Janos (1980), *Economics of Shortage*, London.
- (1987) *Contradictions and Dilemmas: Studies on the Socialist Economy and Society*, Cambridge, Mass., MIT Press.
- (1990), *The Road to a Free Economy. Shifting from a Socialist System: The Case of Hungary*, Norton, New York.
- (1992), *The Socialist System: The Political Economy of Communism*, Princeton University Press, Princeton.
Kotz, David M. (1995), 'Lessons for a Future Socialism from the Soviet Collapse', *Review of Radical Political Economics*, Vol. 27, No. 3, pp. 1-11.
Limia, Miguel (1992), 'La representación laboral en los municipios', (mimeo), Fondo del Instituto de Filosofía, La Habana.
Mandel, Ernest (1986), 'In Defence of Socialist Planning', *New Left Review*, No. 159.
- (1988), 'The Myth of Market Socialism', *New Left Review*, No. 169.
Martín, José Luis (1993), 'La participación de los trabajadores en las empresas', (mimeo), Fondo CIPS, La Habana.
Martín, Juan M. F. (1988), 'Interacciones de los sectores público y privado y la eficiencia global de la economía', *Revista de la CEPAL*, No. 36, Santiago de Chile.
Martínez, Fernando (1993), 'Desconexión, reinserción y socialismo en Cuba; *Cuadernos de Nuestra América*, Vol. X, No. 20, July-Dec., CEA, La Habana.
Mesa Lago, Carmelo (1993), 'The Social Safety Net in the Two Cuban Transitions', in *Cuba in Transition. Study prepared by Florida International University for US Department of State*.
MINFAR (1989), Grupo de Perfeccionamiento de las Organizaciones Empresa riales e Instituciones del MINFAR, *Bases Generales del Perfeccionamiento en el MINFAR*, La Habana.
Monreal, Pedro and Rúa, Manuel (1993), 'Apertura y reforma de la economía cubana', *Cuadernos de Nuestra América*, Vol. X, No. 21, July-Dec.

Moreno, Juan Luis (1993), 'Una pólitica o un sistema monetario óptimo', in *Cuba in Transition*, Vol. 3, Florida International University, Miami.

Nove, Alec (1983), *The Economics of Feasible Socialism*, Allen & Unwin, London.

– (1987), 'Markets and Socialism', *New Left Review*, No. 161.

Pastor, Manuel and Andrew Zimbalist (1995), 'Waiting for Change: Adjustment and Reform in Cuba', *World Development*, Vol. 23, No. 5.

Pazos, Felipe (1992), 'Problemas Económicos de Cuba en el Período de Transición', in George P. Montalván (ed.), in *Cuba in Transition. Volume 1: Papers and Proceedings of the Second Annual Meeting of the Association for the Study of the Cuban Economy*, Miami, Florida International University.

Pérez, Armando and González, Berto (1988), 'El perfeccionamiento empresarial en el MINFAR', *Cuba Socialista*, No. 36, Nov.-Dec.

– (1990), 'La organización de la producción en el perfeccionamiento empresarial de las FAR', *Cuba Socialista*, No. 44, April-June.

Pérez, Armando, Lamar, Lázaro and González, Berto (1989), 'El perfeccionamiento de los sistemas de costos en el MINFAR', *Cuba Socialista*, No. 40, July-Aug.

Pérez-López, Jorge (1991), 'Economic Reform in Cuba: Lessons from Eastern Europe', mimeo, April.

– (1993), 'Learning from Others: Economic Reform Experiences in Eastern Europe, Latin America and China', in *Cuba in Transition. Study prepared by Florida International University for US Department of State*.

Przeworski, Adam (1989), 'Class, Production and Politics: A Reply to Buraway', *Socialist Review*, No. 2.

– (1991), *Democracy and Markets: Political and Economic Reforms in Eastern Europe and Latin America*, Cambridge, Cambridge University Press.

Roca, Sergio (1993), 'Cuban Privatization: Potential Path and Implementation', in *Cuba in Transition. Study prepared by Florida International University for US Department of State*.

Roemer, John E. (1995), *Un futuro para el socialismo*, Editorial Crítica, Madrid.

Rosenbluth, Guillermo (1994), 'Informalidad y pobreza en América Lati na', *Revista de la CEPAL*, No. 92, April.

Salazar, José Manuel (1991), 'El papel del estado y el mercado en el desarrollo económico', in *El desarrollo desde dentro. Un enfoque neoestructuralista para América Latina*, Fondo de Cultura Económica, México.

Sanguinetty, Jorge (1992), 'El Desarrollo de una Economía de Mercado: el Caso de Cuba', in George P. Montalván (ed.), in *Cuba in Transition. Volume 1: Papers and Proceedings of the Second Annual Meeting of the Association for the Study of the Cuban Economy*, Miami, Florida International University.

– (1993), 'The Transition Towards a Market Economy in Cuba: Its Legal and Managerial Dimensions', in *Cuba Transition. Study prepared by Florida International University for US Department of State*.

Solchaga, Carlos (1994), 'La transición cubana', *Actualidad Económica*, 17 Oct., Madrid.

Suárez Salazar, Luis (1993), 'Crisis, restructuración y democracia en Cuba: apuntes para un debate', *Cuadernos de Nuestra América*, Vol. X, No. 20, July-Dec., CEA, La Habana.

Svejnar, Jan and Pérez-López, Jorge (1993), 'A Strategy for the Economic Transformation of Cuba based on The East European Experience', in Carmelo Mesa Lago (ed.), *Cuba After the Cold War*, Pittsburgh, University of Pittsburgh Press.

Tidrick, Gene and Jiyuan, Chen (eds.) (1987), *China's Industrial Reform*, New York, Oxford University Press for the World Bank.

Unanue, Alberto and Rúa, Manuel (1987), 'Reflexiones sobre el papel del tipo de cambio en la economía cubana', *El Economista*, Asociación Nacional de Economistas de Cuba, La Habana.

Valdés Paz, Juan (1993), 'La transición socialista en Cuba: cambio y continuidad', in *La transición socialista en Cuba*, Editorial Colihue, Buenos Aires.

– (1995a), 'Democracia y sistema político', in *Cuba en las Américas. Una perspectiva sobre Cuba y los problemas hemisféricos*, Centro de Estudios sobre América, La Habana.

– (1995b), 'Notas sobre el sistema político cubano', in *La democracia en Cuba y el diferendo con los Estados Unidos*, Centro de Estudios sobre América, La Habana.

Vernon, Raymond (1989), 'Aspectos conceptuales de la privatización', *Revista de la CEPAL*, No. 37, Santiago de Chile.

Weber, Max (1972), *Economía y sociedad*, Editorial de Ciencias Sociales, La Habana.